THE BEST AUSTRALIAN
POEMS
20
17

THE BEST AUSTRALIAN
POEMS

EDITED BY SARAH HOLLAND-BATT

Black Inc.

Published by Black Inc.,
an imprint of Schwartz Publishing Pty Ltd
Level 1, 221 Drummond Street
Carlton VIC 3053, Australia
enquiries@blackincbooks.com
www.blackincbooks.com

9781863959629 (paperback)
9781925435917 (ebook)

Cover design by Peter Long
Typesetting by Tristan Main

Printed in Australia by McPherson's Printing Group.

FSC
www.fsc.org
MIX
Paper from
responsible sources
FSC® C001695

Contents

*　　*　　*

Introduction

Science has recently proven something that most poetry readers already know intuitively to be true: we read poems differently than other kinds of texts. Using fMRI technology, cognitive neurologists at Exeter University scanned the brains of volunteers as they read slabs of dreary prose from a heating installation manual, emotional passages from novels, and their favourite poems. Unsurprisingly, the heating manual failed to light up the part of the brain responsible for sending shivers down the spine. Poetry did, as did lyrical prose. Of particular interest, though, is what happened when participants read their favourite poems: the brain's memory centres were activated more strongly than the areas associated with reading. Rereading our favourite poems, the study suggests, is also an act of remembering.

Two years of editing *The Best Australian Poems* has driven this fact home to me. Reading thousands of poems in a short time span does not sound, on the face of things, particularly conducive to retaining much. And it is true that in the last frenetic months of finalising this selection, I have forgotten car keys, appointments, names, dates, the year. Poetry has sandblasted just about everything else clean out of my head. Yet, even in the midst of this avalanche of reading, I have been surprised by how quickly my favourite lines have earwormed their way into my mind: Todd Turner's description of a horse's shadow 'dense as almond wood', Judith Beveridge's 'crystal brew / of stars' or Julie Chevalier's seagulls that 'stir fry the air', to quote a glittering few. These electric images spring to mind, unbidden, at odd and mundane moments. They accompany me everywhere I go. They insinuate themselves. They insist. I could go on quoting such lines from this year's anthology ad infinitum, but I will leave such gems for readers to discover on their own instead.

In reaching this selection, I have privileged individual poems, not poets. The poems collected here have no preordained shape, subject matter or form. They range from formal verse, where part of the reader's pleasure is in the musical structures of language, to something akin to a jazz riff, where zigs and zags of thought run wild. They blossom from a strange miscellany of subject matter, too: corpse flowers and craft beer tastings populate these pages, as do pigeons trapped inside the dome of the Hagia Sophia, Anna Karenina, cloud formations in Sydney, a plague of bogong moths invading Parliament House, the Borroloola Rodeo and Mahler. Some poems tap into the pop culture zeitgeist and speak in the lexicon of tweets, memes and emojis. Others turn their attention to urgent political, social and environmental issues: the after-effects of the nuclear tests at Maralinga; the spectre of terrorism in Europe; the shock and awe tactics of a bombastic new US president; domestic violence; the UK's protracted and messy exit from the European Union; the role of the element cobalt in building dirty bombs; and the painful legacy of sexual abuse perpetrated by elements of the Catholic Church. And others yet are simply a linguistic joyride at great speed, the poet slaloming around one linguistic hairpin turn after another. In one way or another, they are all highly memorable.

An anthology devoted to the poems of a particular year is bound to display some eclecticism. Poems brush up against one another that would rarely appear in the same company elsewhere. It goes without saying that any other editor would have reached a different combination of 'best' poems than I did; this idea inheres in this anthology's rotating editorship. Even so, I believe these poems offer the best of Australian poetry, in their intelligence and wit, their solace and provocation, their formal genius, their charged encounters with language, and their refusal of all that is ordinary and utilitarian. I found these qualities evident in poems by emerging poets as well as eminent ones; readers will find both here. Some poets whose work I admire greatly are absent by simple virtue of the year's brackets; they have had a fallow year. Others have made a return appearance because they are on a tear at the moment. At the end of the editing process, I was pleasantly surprised to discover that roughly half of the poets here were not present in last year's anthology; this is evidence of the hundreds of serious poets writing in Australia at present. Whittling my selection down to these final hundred poems was difficult, if not downright heartbreaking. The joy and curse of editing an anthology like this is that you become attached to many more poems than you are able to include. To the poets who feel I have let one through to the keeper by skipping over one of their best: I am keenly aware of my own sins of omission. I read many more excellent poems than I was able to publish. This dazzling crop is a sampling, not a complete edition.

As I did last year, I must applaud all the literary journals, magazines, newspapers and other venues that publish poems in this country, as well as the small and independent presses that are its lifeblood, especially given the current publishing climate. It is quite incredible to contemplate the collective effort, dedication and sheer force of will that brought all of the thousands of poems I read this past year to print. In the midst of all this energetic publishing activity, however, this past year also shepherded in a few sad developments. I know I am not alone in feeling disheartened that stalwarts the *Age* and the *Sydney Morning Herald* have shuttered their weekly publication of poetry. Many major Australian poems first appeared in those pages, where they jostled for attention with statecraft, economics and sport: an incongruous but oddly fitting context for poetry which, like reportage, illuminates world and self. Here's hoping the *Weekend Australian* and the *Canberra Times* continue printing poems.

Over the course of my reading, I came across a few special projects that I would like to recommend to readers. Martin Langford, Judith Beveridge, Judy Johnson and David Musgrave co-edited the monumental *Contemporary Australian Poetry*, a lively survey volume which is well worth the price of admission. Heather Taylor Johnson edited *Shaping the Fractured Self: Poetry of Chronic Illness and Pain*, an incisive collection of poems and essays offering a view into the body in trauma. And John Kinsella and Tracy Ryan edited *The Fremantle Press Anthology of Western Australian Poetry*, canvassing poetry from the nineteenth century to the present, including a substantial number of Indigenous poets from the region. Beyond these excellent publications, however, I would encourage readers to buy the individual collections of the poets they have particularly enjoyed here; this is the best way to support poets and the tireless editors and presses who publish them.

This anthology opens with a poem by the late poet Fay Zwicky, who passed away only one day after the publication of her masterful *Collected Poems*, assiduously edited by Lucy Dougan and Tim Dolan. Zwicky wrote some of the most compelling Australian poems of the past century, including her magisterial elegy for her father, *Kaddish*, wherein she upended the gender roles of her Jewish heritage by invoking the Kaddish prayer as a woman, an act proscribed by the Jewish faith. There have been a number of affecting tributes examining Zwicky's manifold contributions to Australian letters published since her death in July, with more, I am sure, to follow; in these pages, Barry Hill remembers her in his eloquent 'Mister Lincoln or Camp David'. Zwicky is represented here by another elegy, her final published poem, 'In Memoriam, JB', a bravura work that closes with characteristically clear-eyed, profound lines: 'We only ever yield to love / when someone's dead or gone.'

This past year also saw the passing of Rae Desmond Jones, a much-loved Sydney poet, novelist, short-story writer, and one-time popular mayor of the inner-Sydney municipality of Ashfield. With John Edwards, Jones founded and edited the long-running iconoclastic journal *Your Friendly Fascist*, known for its irreverence and joyful anarchism. Jones's own poetry was likewise relentlessly inventive, propulsive and often satirical; his writing life was marked by what John Jenkins aptly described as a long-waged 'campaign against dullness, comfortable formulas and poetic complacency.' Jones, like Zwicky, is remembered with great affection by the many poets and fellow publishers to whom he was a generous mentor and friend. He closes this anthology with a moving poem from his final collection of ghazals, the superb *A Caterpillar on a Leaf* (Puncher & Wattman), where the poet confronts death with a light touch.

Also included in this volume is a poem by the late John Upton, poet, dramatist and screenwriter, who staged numerous plays over his career, as well as writing for more than twenty Australian television series, before devoting his retirement to poetry. Upton published one poetry collection in 2014, *Embracing the Razor* (Puncher & Wattman), and is represented in this anthology with a nimble travel poem published this past year, 'Crossing Galata, Istanbul', in which the poet stands among fishermen on the Galata Bridge over the Golden Horn, watching the 'rods bowing and bobbing' until he experiences a complex transmogrification from human and animal, passing 'between poles / of then and now, / a fish caught / in a rip of time.' It's a deft performance that gets more strange and wondrous on each rereading.

Finally, to all the poets collected in this volume: thank you for your company over this year of reading; it's been a gift to spend so much time with your poems. I am also grateful to Black Inc. for its enduring commitment to this important series, and, by extension, to Australian poetry. I must give special thanks to Chris Feik for the invitation to edit *The Best Australian Poems* these past two years; I've enjoyed every minute of it, even the most difficult of deliberations. Thanks, too, to Erin Sandiford and Siân Scott-Clash for their considerable help in making these two anthologies happen. And to the readers of *The Best Australian Poems 2017*, I hope you see in these poems what I see: order and rebellion, ardour and irony, beauty and abjection and everything in between.

Sarah Holland-Batt

In Memoriam, JB

You're leaving us
the things you found (we found) so hard
to speak about—the books, the films,
the high beam on your car, political shenanigans
that split us wide apart, the things we never
could agree upon, you on the right,
me on the left.

I well recall the night before the Iraq invasion
shouting at you over quaking scallopini at Valdarno's
tears streaming down my face, specs all misted over—
can't you see?
can't you see?
why won't you see?

And you, polite, calm, infuriatingly right,
the tactful English gentleman confronting
the unruly desperate Australian virago.
What's the matter with the woman?

True grief is tongueless (as I once said
in an earlier poem about lost love).
I still believe it.
We never learn, dear John.
We've grown up like a pack of frightened kids
standing in the corners of the world,
graduates of the school of inhibition, cum laude,
wary of weapons of mass destruction,
the biggest of which is death.

We're learning ...

We feared that love was not enough.
You doubted your own goodness.
We never did. But now are left
to linger guilty in your debt.

We only ever yield to love
when someone's dead or gone.

Fay Zwicky

Winter, Hospital Bed

Memory was the room I entered down a long corridor
Thrown by the white drugs of pain though pain
Was adrift on a glassy stream of green tide
Where images flickered and ran on

I didn't write poetry for publication
In those days but to grab the attention
Of readers nearby who had been crushed by life
Who floated across the exercise yard like headaches

Smoking rag-cigarettes looking sideways
For the next punishment for a break or maybe distraction
Chips of memory kept rising to the surface
Of our minds to take another bite

I had no idea why poetry the squid caught me
It clung to my brain in the damaging climate
A creature in the alien element of air
Arising from centuries of survival

Thoughts must be inky and capable
Of working the bait with a black beak
For a quick kill and a metaphysical rise up through the abyss
Poetry in those days was a hand-made lure

There were no fish or birds so I spun my lines
To the ones with heads spring-loaded with resentment
Their temper a red-fleck twitching in an eye
While poems of the future waited in line to hear my number

Robert Adamson

cobalt

Co—nclusion: following find in 1982 by local sponge diver
Mehmed Çakir & 11 campaigns {over 22 000 descends} the
Uluburun drowned in the Mediterranean Sea at the end of
the 14th century BC {see golden scarab inscribed 'Nefertiti'} &
amongst other treasures of this Late Bronze Age trove   a
single ingot of pure blue glass   proving such perfectness lasts

from Persia & Pompeii to Tang & Ming to the Congo
& Zambia belt   you are my plenary blue   at rest upon
fingers   tables of kings   you make love with eyes   make
cats made of stone stare back   this is when I love you
best   one stable isotope   11 meta states   a church where
the Virgin locks out shock & we're safe   but sometimes
the door divorces its hinge & Kobold the Goblin gets
a foot in   o wobbly-wobbly-precarious-psyche   stories
packed with dirty bomb endings   everything starts to
turn black   sometimes you weep way down within &
your tears fall silent like gamma ray ash   your grief can
wipe out the world   sometimes you wail like a doomsday
device   emit a steady sad-sad pulse   but you always mend
& you always return   & you always remind no matter how
hurt that "Mutual Assured Destruction" spells the word/
world   mad

Jordie Albiston

Gypsy

You come from a family of boys. I come from no family at all. My great-grandmother was born with holes in her earlobes. Romany. Gypsy. A caravan child. I remember my childhood of Russian Caravan Tea, all lapsang souchong-y. You think Gypsy means Gypsy Rose Lee and regale me with stories of her speaking at Union Meetings. I wait for the striptease. We run away to Coney Island. I thought it would be all yellow neon ice-cream cones before we take the D train to Brooklyn. But my dreams short circuit. There is no Copacabana or Tropicana. No birthday cakes like the ones I dreamt about in the *Women's Weekly* cookbook. Coney Island is *Nathan's Famous Hotdogs* not Rapunzel's tower made of inverted cones covered in cream. You take me to the boardwalk but never under it. I take you to the sideshow where the bearded lady reads your tea leaves and points out the long plait curling itself around the rim of your cup.

Cassandra Atherton

Reunion Song

Every time she saw herself in the mirror, I remember, she push-
ed her chin forwards so as to stretch the skin of her neck. The
crushed tram ticket in her throat produced the crumpled husky
sound itself. She had seen a throat specialist at one point and
I told her a long anecdote about my trip to NY, which fanned
out from the phrase 'detective work' which I used to describe
my absorption in research. I sat there, in the library, for 9 hours
a day, a short lunch in the brisk sub-zero sun, and spoke to her
of the blizzard and its pattern on the east coast. A doctor point-
ed the sharp beak of curlew at her neck which twitched like
a nerve as she sang: it's nearly 10! We had had another wine
and met outside the pain – 7 years. Most of the local bars
were closed and the cellar was closed to the public given a wh-
isky festival. I stirred honey into the corner of my mouth and
went to itch my own brain through a hole in the back of my
skull obscured by a flap of thick hair. The texture of a soccer
ball retrieved from a swamp, my mind. Colour of cross trainers,
lycra. She'd been an avid runner. It's harder to communicate
the evening without thinking about breakup (ours) and death
(her mother's) but we used those words. The light was very low.

Luke Beesley

Flying Foxes, Wingham Brush

For Deborah Bird Rose

Some of the bats are elbowing their way
along the branches, a collection of broken
business umbrellas. Some hang like charred

pods, or look like furry oriental fruit
wrapped in silk sashes. Others are handling
the stretch of their black elastomer wings

as carefully as women checking for snags
in their stockings, ready to step out for the night.
But the smell of the place—decades

of urine, faeces, birth fluids, rotting body
parts and figs, putrid as a munitions factory
with its cloying nitrates, its biting ammonia.

At dusk when the bats take off, the sky
becomes a long sheet of gothic lettering—
some won't return, they'll swing by their

feet on highwires, doomed stuntmen
still in their leathers. Newly-orphaned bats,
grief-stricken, will roost on Hills hoists,

snuggle against the lingerie and socks,
the sharp metal squeaks sounding like calls
from their mothers. Some believe bats

are demons' hand puppets, the souls of
unburied infants, death-messengers nibbling
at the edges of our dreams, but I love to listen

to them sending out their clicks and squeaks,
flying under the moon, the crystal brew
of stars; how after sweeping upwards, they'll

backtrack to parks, yards, hearing all the angles
and contours in our gardens, soliloquising
their way through tunnels and labyrinths,

weighing their love of nectar with the love
of night-flight—scent-resonators
of the season. Now high in these branches

they're as chatty as children fuelled by
afternoon sugars. They hug themselves lightly,
closely, the way tree-lovers hug wood.

Judith Beveridge

The Grey Parrot

After the painting The Grey Parrot by Walter Deverell,
National Gallery of Victoria

The far city must make itself known
even here in the sitting room and
barred by winter branches. The skyline

with its towers square as pillars
built of blocks could be here
as much as then and there and is

in any case beyond hearing.
Long withdrawn from the city
that oversees life to a home

where rapt stillness is a cultivated
guest and the ghost of light
leavens the chores of daily bread,

she would come to lend her features
to ideas she understood
could be treated most faithfully

in art that generates no
propulsion other than
this same descent into pleasure

gently shared between minds
– those branched apart by
evolution, or merely space and time

Judith Bishop

Time is a river, time is a bridge

Time is a river that passes through you, crossing and
recrossing, rippling score of silence under the bridges of your
life, and you wonder if it can be the same river or the same
person twice, the amber glide of the Arno, the spring light
polished in memory, a long scroll of plainsong flowing out of
some deep medieval past, and I am back here in middle age,
mid-river, the Ponte Vecchio downstream a golden span, a
bridge crossed a lifetime ago, sniffing out echoes of that early
spring morning when our steps rang out softly on the stone
streets on the other side of the river, our first morning in
this city that seems to go in search of itself, piazza by piazza,
church by church. In the hostel kitchen Ansgar had said,
"That is why I come back every year, the beautiful stone alleys
and hidden gardens." Each spring he made his way here from
Skagen, after his wife's death. His words came slow, the Nordic
accent laden, as though they were slow steps in heavy snow.
After breakfast he led us, shuffling in leather loafers worn as
his face, through quiet streets of shuttered windows and arched
doors, the stone alleys that gave nothing away, the April light
shifting with each turn, brightening the top of the buildings,
parleying with the counterpointing shade, foreshortening and
then lengthening perspective. Ansgar moved so slow it was as
if he wanted us to read the unwritten history of the city, the
journal our steps traced on the rivers of worn stone. The old
man's drooping mouth curled in a child's smile as he ushered
us through a gate. To a pause in time. And we sat at the
fountain in the cloistered garden, ringed by arched galleries of
a convent. Ansgar held out a brown paper bag, the tremor in
his hands at breakfast gone, his fingers gnarled, skin thickened
from a life trade in carpentry. The cherries sparkled in the
chant of light and water, and we ate without a word, on our
foreign tongue the dark crimson flesh turning into sweet wine.

And the pale blue light in Ansgar's eyes answered the chords
of the Florentine sun, the peace settling on his face like Victor
Sjöström's in *Wild Strawberries*, the peace that had travelled a
long way from home, from the pine forests in the deep north,
the hidden fjords of Ansgar's life, from the past, from its glide
into the future, travelling through the seasons to hold this gate
in time open.

***

Time is a bridge you cross and recross, the river's song
unchanged in memory's burnish and in your mind's reliquary
this frayed image of the naked Christ, the pale sheen of its
slender carved body suspended in space, calling from the
sacristy of lost time, that spring morning when Ansgar led us
to the plain Romanesque façade of the Santo Spirito. In the
nave we stood, still in the hull of a submarine ark, and felt the
press of silence, emptiness contained, and then the distant
hum, long deep waves of soundings, till like struck bells, we
heard it ring on and on within us, calling us to step across
the threshold, through the door in the aisle to the sacristy,
the life-size crucifix bathed in the floating panes of light from
the apse windows, hung by a thick wire rope. Naked Christ,
not even a crown of thorns or a modest loincloth, his long
slender arms held up as if in flight, the right foot nailed on
top of the other foot, so the knee and hip are canted to the
left, in counterpoint to the right tilt of the downcast head, its
finely chiselled hippie face and eyes closed in the perfection of
death. No hint of resurrection, this quiet death coming to life
under the sculpting knife, unpeeled to the mortal light. Such
perfection learned from anatomising corpses from the basilica
hospital when Michelangelo found refuge here at seventeen.
You wonder about the young man he picked to be this serene
Christ, the body still garbed in its mortal dress of joy or pain,
coiled in pain or taut in lust, not this loose-limbed pinioned

repose. We bowed before its beauty, then bought postcards from the basilica shop. For years the dead face was taped to the wall above my study desk, till it vanished in the move to another country, another life from yours. And each Florentine spring Ansgar sent a postcard to you, then silence. Time is a river you recross, ford to the place you have been before, the past coming alive on the other shore. Memory's guesswork, crossing another bridge, from the Duomo side, my feet feeling these streets without a map, as Ansgar's did, trusting memory's route, drifting past the open market, the morning light now warming the tree-lined piazza and the face of the Santo Spirito, streaming through the high windows to find us standing in the sacristy, dipped in the font of silence, as if in the vault of held prayer, before the hanging, waiting body.

Kim Cheng Boey

Reach & Ambition

For John Jenkins

I Reach & Ambition

Late at night, up, looking at
the things on my mantelpiece
a profusion of crap, clutter & gewgaws
a range of detail I love (John's photos of it
came today, reminding me). I look at the pictures
blu-tacked there, above—postcards of paintings
1900 to 1920s mostly
but some Manet, some Fragonard, a Boucher
Michael Fitzjames, a Chardin—a piece of paper,
yellowed, proclaiming "*Honeymooners* star
Meadows dies" (with a picture of Art
Carney, Gleason, & Meadows), a picture
of James Brown being 'assisted'
to his feet
by a Famous Flame, a large photocopy picture
of Pam, 32 or 3 … Anyway, the Manet—
two white camellias glowing
against a black ground—makes me think
Look at things! & on that basis
I think I will search out
the book of Manet's flower-pieces
& then, depending what that does to my brain,
re-read the Tranter poem I find,
placed in the back of this book. 'Loxodrome'.
And maybe I will

II Gone

                    Left of the mantelpiece,
beneath the Chardin (a small, be-suited,
silver-haired boy—regarding a spinning top
on the table before him), four
tiny spots,
of blu-tack,
form a rectangle
where a stamp should be—a patch of torn envelope
& the postal stamp that was on it. Gone. John's photos,
tho, reveal it to have featured a dalek.
U.K. recognition for *Dr Who*. I am relieved.
For months now I have been aware
of the missing stamp, & had looked about for it,
thinking it showed a Chance Vought
Corsair, a fighter aeroplane of WWII
that I had liked. ('Liked'.) I had been a fan of the plane
in my teens—& surprised to receive its image
as an adult forty years later stuck on an envelope,
& looking so American, mid-century & 'of its era'.
I don't know who had sent it to me
tho there are only a few candidates.
But now I see it is only a dalek—was only a dalek—
& I care *nothing* for *Dr Who*. The fighter plane
will show up one day, within a book of poems,
marking a spot to return to—in O'Hara or
Towle or Berrigan, Padgett or Mathews—
& I will be surprised & admire it for a second

III (Further)

       Further right—
beyond a photo, from the outside,
of the front of the house at Westbury Street,
where I lived nine years—a photo
Mary gave me, the house white, window-sill
& door pale blue, maybe the fancy iron lacework
at the eave below the guttering blue too
the whole framed by the green leaves of a tree,
the wood of the tree an angled dark accent
at the right ... Anyway, near it
are some designs of mine, screenprinted
or water-coloured, & some pictures, with figures
(it occurs to me now)
grouped in threes.
One, rather Pop, shows a mother & father
clean-cut, at a restaurant, flanking their son—
the cartoon 'Burt' from *The Muppets* who looks
straight at us, while Mom & Dad look right,
alert to ... a nightclub act? a waiter?—
something outside the picture. Of course
Burt looks bizarre. Above, women clean up the Reichstag
after WWII—three women, it appears—in fact
three pairs of women—bend, mopping or shovelling
at rubble, dark figures, shapeless,
dwarfed by the immensely tall
pale Greek columns of the ruined building.
Beside Burt & his parents, a photo from late 19th Century:
"The Match-girls' strike: their pay was docked
to erect a statue of Mr Gladstone" says the caption.
High-waisted skirts & tight, formal blouses,
all with hats—their best clothes—one looks pretty
& all look aggrieved & sure of their cause—
then a Braque or Picasso abstract—smudged,
glowing grey, & brown, & white, of a kind called (once?)
                      hermetic

IV 'Loxodrome'

John's poem, John Tranter's poem, 'Loxodrome', I was
about to call it 'Lucasade', is great.
On first reading I was conscious
mostly of its easily maintained urbanity
& its complexity, charting a move
from North to Southern hemisphere—
in a corkscrew motion?—via visits to certain
'places'—New York, Paris, Australia—
& poetic *spaces*—Baudelaire, Ashbery-&-O'Hara,
Forbes—& to poetry readings & events, & then
his response. It includes two pieces of
information I recall giving John, knowing they
were his kind of thing—about Freud
& Arthur Hugh Clough. Now I read the poem
closely for the sense & grammar
of the construction. Good to have that clear.
In the poem John imagines me
spying on him thru the fence—as
he cleans the pool, pointing out
annoyingly, a leaf he has missed?
Then John Forbes, in JT's dream,
notes an error in one of his poems.
In fact, I see a change that could be usefully made
myself, tho not necessary & I doubt
I'd point it out. "(R)ecalls, for us, a tireless
mechanical rocking horse / galloping evenly
over the heather, the rhythm / soothing
& slightly narcotic." Would that be better?
Maybe not much. Maybe not at all.

V The things JJ liked

The things that John must've liked—
(tho he liked it all, the confusion)—
at one end of the mantelpiece a small yellow
monoplane, high-winged, its propeller & wheels
of a like yellow—an infant's toy—one wheel
a little broken. It sits, like everything, wedged in,
between jars & dishes (of paper clips, pencils), pencil
    sharpeners (*one*
—one of these—in the shape of a nose), small bottles I must
    have liked
—for their shape & colour—two 'metal' milkshake holders
cast actually in ceramic, one with a bunch of pigs-bristle
paint-brushes rising out of it, like flowers from a vase.
The second one (both are mauve) has a small flyer
for a piano recital on Cortula or Hvar.
Ivan Pernicki—tho Ivan Pernikety
I preferred at the time. (It got rained out,
cancelled. We were going to go—the posters were all
over the island: Chopin's mazurkas, I'd like to think.)
                                    In
what looks like a small urn—ceramic tho it pretends to be
                        woven brush—
(coppery orange)—is a perfectly round
white or flesh-coloured ping-pong ball, with
a face painted on it comically menacing & ghoulish
with a black top hat: its amused eyes rest
just above the urn's rim. (It's mounted on
a toothpick, I know, so you could stick it in things
(food? A cake?) & was given to us by Yuri's
then German girlfriend, Kathleen, from Dresden.
We never met: we were overseas: but she liked us—
liked Yuri—& left some presents for the house.
There's a clothes brush I never use. Some stickytapes,

small staplers, a book cover—grey, proof copy—
for Pam's *Fifty-Fifty*. There it is again, nearby,
in 'full' colour, & a vase from my childhood—
& perhaps from Dad's, or did he gain it
as a wedding present?—
a toffee-brown, with a scene painted on it—
people sitting in an 18th century farm kitchen:
tables, chairs, an open fire
a bonneted woman sitting in a niche
against the wall knitting: passing time, but busy.
Back at the other end, near the plane, some
rusched paper snakes—that I think Sally Forth
gave me: they're broken now but still look serpentine—
in fact, even more so. They were attached to sticks,
& almost invisible thread allowed them to move,
snakily. There's a Paul Sloan painting—an image
on a postcard, behind the snakes (just below
Burt *et famille*); there are two Singer sewing machine
'light-oil' containers, why? & a picture by Micky
(Micky Allan), framed, of
a curiously carefree footballer (a goalie, I always think)
failing to make a save. (There are goal posts, pennants,
an indication of a crowd, behind.) Late in the day—
or maybe it's *early* in the game, but it is
how he intends to go on. Right near by,
on the door of the clothes cupboard is a colour photo
(from *The Guardian*) of a guy—on the wing—running
full tilt, the ball (Rugby) clutched high
against his chest, skinny, head thrown back
ecstatic that—by his lights—he's going to make it,
just, in the very corner in a moment. It says,
"David Humphreys scores one of Ulster's two tries"
He looks like he's missing some teeth. You want him
to succeed. The crowd are yelling & laughing.
He could easily be bundled out, you would think,

but he's going to make it. I love it: human frailty
simple pleasures. What else?—Beckmann
(*Lido*). Martha Reeves & the Vandellas (beautiful
in very funny pants) Richard Widmark—
in a sixties suit & hat, narrow tie, pressed flat
against a wall, expectant, gun out—two
Joe Louis postage stamps, Stendhal, pictures by
Kurt, & one by Sal, a photo of The Nips—formerly
The Nipple Erectors—posed in the street, the lead singer
in a zoot suit, slightly crouched, legs apart, the sole
girl in the band amused at the boys' antics
stands very still, holds her guitar, smiles; a drawing I did,
of a hat, for *August 6ᵗʰ*.

                          I did it
here in this room, under the fluoro, at the desk.

                          There's Rauschenberg's
                                    chair—
combined with the painting, & Seb & Mill
& Mill's baby, Hec.

Ken Bolton

Eleutheria

Water spirit of small bowls
beyond the bamboo curtain of my window
a black bowl harbouring green shoots I have no name for
maybe the small slick of water
on the surface
is enough for you
maybe the few early morning raindrops
are enough for you
an ornamental tree spreading fan-like branches
two small stone steps into a garden
with room only for a few
well-tended weeds (if everything non-native
is a weed) sun water
a few flourishes of stone
I would have liked an ocean a tidal inlet
a riverbed at least or clear creek
cut like childhood between suburban allotments
but where you glide is my renewal
telling me a cup will do
a line of silver in air
to swim and glide and curl up
within a water-drop
in the tracery of moisture at the end of a leaf
what this morning the birds harvest in the long
silence of the skies

Peter Boyle

Forty-one degrees

Almost summer, season of hot dry winds.
Cooling off in Clovelly Bay, among
sea-urchins and blue gropers, you enter
          a floating world, easy to forget
out there it's another heatwave.
Outside my townhouse, men with hats
and overheated brains are repairing
     the roof, damaged in last April's storms,
still leaking water.

The garden needs watering. While rock-plants
and veldt daisies may survive
                    into our future desert, magnolias
bloom fast and quickly die, browned flowers
          drifting onto unswept tiles. At dusk
the air's still warm, black cockatoos have fled
with raucous cry, back to their cooler forests.
In a neighbouring pond, frogs belt out
        loud mating-songs, secure for now, until
developers arrive, to move the earth.

Out there, it's also a war on terror
as jihadists and extremists take control
and suddenly we know
                how, at any given moment,
in a train carriage in London, a music festival
in Paris, or a Lindt cafe somewhere
life can be snatched away.
Même pas mal, say the French, in solidarity,
"Not even hurt." But we all are.

In this hot, shifting darkness
                I wish the rains would come.

Margaret Bradstock

The Shower Stall

Wisdom does not follow conquest, although
I tend to fall into thinking so. Sitting here,
on a milk crate, watching the easy bounty

of bore water sluice over her leg, holding
the hose high above her knee, so the current
cascades down slender cannon to film and bulb

the swell of her fetlock and then rush away
over coronet, hoof, concrete floor, to pool among
blue top, farmer's friend, toads, dragonfruit rot, wild

raspberry bushes that house the black, spare
fairy-wrens with their flash of slapstick orange.
A slow sulphur of pain, low and new in my back,

I rest my forehead against her belly, listen
to the secret world of digestion
and the ever present electrics

of a prey animal, tranquillized for now
by the water whispering to her hot leg,
by my hand on her shoulder, but ever alert

just below the surface, like a bream ready
to dart for those insects that sit and skim.
The infection is no worse, nothing has risen

any further. The grass has grown too long,
once the rains have stopped the tractor
will come to slash the paddocks, until then,

the weeds have won. Ants retreat down a fencepost;
flushing the black pepper of grass seed out
of the wound, I feel a shift in pressure

under the iron hull of cloud before
the next deluge. A magpie calls bright and clear in the lull,
teaching its juvenile to hunt, to be,

and a large butterfly appears, solitary, wings the dark
grain of cedar or mahogany. The world ripples
when I stand, unwell, I guess, but not enough

to notice until I'm in the realm of the physical:
paddocks, mud, boots, wheelie bin of chaff
smelling sweeter than cakes never baked

in my childhood oven. Autumn is around the corner
with its mornings of mist and promise
of dry days. The rain, now, when it comes,

is cooler than I expect. It runs down my back
in rivulets, soothes the burr of fever against
my skin. I can no longer see the hills,

all is valley now, all close in. The young
magpie dips and jogs, staccato, across
the round ring, looking for the worm.

Lisa Brockwell

The Night Coming

I was thinking it was cold, the heater
struggling against the draught,
and that there was nothing I could say, how
empty my mind was,
but then looked up and saw you
working in the paddock in the thin rain in your black
jacket against the almost-
evening of the trees
with the white dog at heel
and the four sheep grazing about you
and the sounds, through the mist, of the cockatoos
settling in the high branches,
the woodshed in its winter sleep,
the five wild ducks
moving in single file through the grass.

David Brooks

Soft Targets

the miracle pill
     is a sludge drench

been given the slipperies
        at
        central railway
        & again

    at the airport check in

a useless delay
  adds shadows
    to waiting
        so   last week's
        couple of hours
        at Eddie's cafe -
collards & patties
cornbread & chops

with friends
from some own-private
A-List,

      remodel sentimentally
      as memorable

everything edible
digested then combined
in blood's micro mix -
        dry cleaning fluid
        paint thinners
        toilet deodorisers
        benzene fuel drops

ddt / literal poisons
fish patties
& sweet greens

plus the poison I use
to shrink my virus

*

I can only work
the trap I'm in

*

on the plane
everyone's weeping
at their tiny screens

I weep for Janis   for Amy
for collards & for cornbread

soft targets
up in the air,
softies

you want to set
a favourite diversion -
describe
a spiral staircase
without using gestures

but
can't play that

                    more loving
                  if I could

even for a short time

                        *

lobes drop
  & droop
almost to my collar

                my skull
                must be withering
as
I head
towards my allotted truism

Pam Brown

compensation

excitement   a revised
flyover to choctop
boredom   so let's sip
prosecco like white
chiffon flutologists
how those 3d-eed
bubbles tickle your
fancy   i went to
the wrong movie but
had the right ticket
for an emergency tax
deduction   i'm sorry
i can't remember the
director's name   was it
fellini, bergman, or taran-
tino   everyone seems to rush
out before the credits start
to roll — i'm indebted to
the reliability of an elevator
even if the traffic lights insist
on being stubborn   the spring
water is half the price across
the rheumatoidal road   they call
it tank stream spa   well did you
bring your pack of loyalty cards

Joanne Burns

Minor Domestic

Jacarandas luxuriate
doused at dusk,
a xylography of fringed leaves
combs the barking
light.
Disabled elms sway,
the hedges ungainly, wield
to the drama of day.
A license to renew, the house
aphasic, tangled: missing
marbles, a stapler,
wedge sandals strewn.
A half moon, flesh
flapping from knuckle,
like thumping, a detail:
ruby spurts in her room. How a child
dreams of sea-maidens
in tidal streams
while grown-ups carve
out the silence.

Michelle Cahill

c'est l'homme

for John Forbes

                              you
develope a style until
it can say what you want   you need   it may
take years and years

of need   a style
is a bit like a life
                              and then
it comes together
style   book   life
                              and then
much to your surprise
this neat construction
falls apart

there is no book
the life is not what was planned
and the style
seems hopelessly out of date and
immortality a fading dream but

the need
turns out to be timeless

and in the house there is
some small drug or other
to tide you over
                              and the style
takes a mini cooper and throws it
down like a gauntlet

and choosing a word is again
the first mouthful of something
brilliant and daring
always perfect

                      and you know
despite all the stumbling about in the bushes
the stubbed toes   the dirt   the broken fingernails

there was a kind of twisted little track
leading to the photo opportunity at the top of the cliff
and from there you can see

a mini cooper burning in the snow

perfect

Lee Cataldi

another step away

in homage to frank o'hara

a fix of toby's estate coffee on the footpath.
baird has sold the education department
& another heritage building:
archival storage boxes re-labelled 'wine glasses'

past the museum of sydney—martin sharp's
tunnel of love—rows of ancestral totems
names of the dead as mournful
as first people circular breathing down at the quay

the art of war is showing at the gallipoli club
the bar girl winks   her cubes
languorously agitating   a man slumps on the door
of a soon-to-open restaurant

around the corner gulls stir fry the air
someone in a sari hurries
towards the noodles of bridge street
the sun is hot   a silver statue stifles a sneeze

outside customs house   buskers on unicycles
juggle flames & gimme signs
at wharf six   captain cook
directs travellers to the bondi explorer

the infirm struggle to board 'the radiance of the sea'
ferries turn beneath a jacaranda sky
the harbour arch crawls with climbers
in search of a mountain

outside the mca rows of green tufts implanted
on bald ground   a baby magpie is fed
shredded lettuce   a man in a hoodie competes
with ibises for poly-boxes in bins

in the rocks five maseratis & two passengers
dressed in ribbons & lavender fur
halt all traffic without permission:
the importance of filming their music video

yellow helmets protect labourers from talkback radio
it's my lunch hour, so i go

Julie Chevalier

Kumera

Wrap whole sweet potatoes,
skin on, in foil. Place among
the embers of coals – long after

the chicken wings and satay
have run out: the tender, orange
flesh of the kumera – steaming

in the night air, smoky skin
peeled off in strips. One winter,
in Kunming, ascending the path

to the Dragon's Gate, a woman
standing watch over an oil drum.
Scent of sweet potatoes cooking –

men devouring its meat by the roadside.
In the war it was all that would grow
in the gardens, fertilised by shit.

I ask my mother for rice porridge
boiled with kumera. This thin gruel:
the bright, cubed gifts of our survival.

Eileen Chong

Two Women

Believe nothing she says. Provide her with a warm coat.
Believe nothing she says. Give her a cigarette, and a light.

Believe nothing she says. When her foot is trapped, stoop,
wrestle with the slab until it yields. Then caress the mark.

Wait for her, wait for her, wait for her two hours before
you give up. Hear out the reasons that she gives with

equanimity. There will be reasons, of course there are.
Believe nothing she says. She isn't lying, you wouldn't

call it lying, but it is an artful art. A kind of inveiglement.
The inconstant narrative of bewilderment. She shivers but

she's not cold, she says. It's winter and we are all cold.
It's cold. But fold away the facts, put them in your pocket.

This is a labyrinth, with a broken thread. Feel about in the
muck, in the dark, for the two frayed ends and make a knot.

It might hold. Or it won't. Beat fists against your forehead.
Confess. You yourself have been dissonant with grief. Why

you write this. Late at night, jangled, without recourse to
irony or impatience or display, at least insofar as that goes.

You yourself would have tried the patience of a saint. So
do anything for her except believe anything that she says.

Jennifer Compton

Fallen Myrtle Trunk

in the temperate forests, the wet
        sclerophyll forests, where the wind
                moans in yourm leaves, a storm beating
                        in muffled drums at the entrance
                                to the underworld, the lands
                                        of Gondwana, motherland of Australia,
                                                South America, the hundreds
                                                        of years creeping, the moss about youm creeping
                                                        the growling thunder, the black sou'-wester
                                                        —by youm all this recedes, falls
                                                        like wilting springs

                                                        aged into agelessness, less
                                                        than age, giant
                                                        fullness, monoforest
                                                        bulk
                                                        of years and slowness
                                                        hint of snake while touch crumbles
                                                        like chocolate flakes, vibration vanishes
                                                        in yourm tomb, tombing
                                                        yourm slumber rots, beachwards
                                                        a giant petrified in light

                                                        imperceptible scuttle scattered
                                                        deeply, cavern hymns at
                                                         cave hertz, yourm august
                                                            specific music, cylindrical fugue
                                                                of dark brown scales, closed soft pink
                                                                    to reddish grain, edified with mountain
                                                                        ash memory, guardian of closed passage
                                                                            pillar of larger sky, of facts like clouds
                                                                                        their sky ways wending

youm known the songs of lonely places
the ways of wet and wind, youm moan
of fire, unless the flames come slowly
for yourm return to drowsy
droning, the intoning
of the wizard priests
the sough of the southern seas
youm're the stage before the sea
the ground's stage, for all sea-yearning

yourm limbed stances
form too slowly for change, beneath
such gestures the black flock shelters, shadowed
in yourm underside, that invisible realm
of canal venom and webbed vein

to the light youm present carpet bridge, seedling
lives held by yourm unfolding descent, dark-
plumed monarch, ebony laced
with wing, by the mountain rills
down to the parched saplings
on the shore of a receding lake
youm know too much
of that escarpment beyond, rest
pray, yourm beast prepares for return

while everything frizzes, shifts
     brushed and squeeze, sway
          youm remain sound-
               like, a solid gradient an always
                    line, travelling
                         and unravelling through the same place

                    yourm skin mimics lake ripple
                    grooved rivulets criss-cross like thickened years
                    currents of stone into softer solid
                    edging damp, ripples merged with moss
                    the land's dry, soft with moss
                    a surface of crawling speckleds, blood legs and
                    black bodies, orange-like
                     fruiting bodies protruding from
                       yourm furry, whaled bulk

                         moss colony, moss scape, the stick shade
                              of a seedling wobbles
                                   on yourm chest flecked with sonnet,leaf voltas
                                        their dark green, lost brilliance

then fresh reds, pinked to orange faded
    ragged, triangled teeth
        and fruits of three small
            winged nuts, subtle flourish
                of yellow-green catkins, now a mouthing
                    eddy where a bough broke off
                        airborne spores of wilt lulled by such knots
                        have settled on yourm wound

                one branch, there, pleads help
                by reaching, others
                    arch hardened spines around gravity's slide
                    while youm host the epiphytes
                        while the termites elaborate
                            yourm runnelled intentions
                                while moss slowly fingers, surrounds
                                    slowly devours these juts of twig
                                        slowly devours its own ground
                                                which youm perform patiently for it

Stuart Cooke

'Fallen Myrtle Trunk' contains echoes of the following poems:
'Mountain Myrtle', by Marie E. J. Pitt
'Out of Sorts and Looking at Elms', by Simon West

meadows empty of him, animal eyes,
impersonal as glass

Aubades

to be a part of the outward life, to be out there at the edge of
things, to let the human taint wash away in emptiness and silence
as the fox sloughs his smell in the cold unworldliness of water.
—J.A. Baker

1.
There is the time before the knowing.
When I see the fox, and stop
my breath.
It is so light on the path –
there will be no pawprints in the hard
earth. Rain drifts
grainily in
the air, but I have felt nothing
on my skin for hours. It is the time, after
all, before the knowing,

which is not time, but the pausing of it.
It trots towards me, noses
the wet under-
brush, keeping to the edges
of the path, delicate as the breath not
taken, the unmoving
air, that must
have moved – since it starts,
and scents in me what I've not sensed,
the deepest predatory

wish; that I want only to pin it down, bury
my face in its winter fur.
Struck now:
my knowing of it will be the worst
of all deaths. It skips
sideways
from the path. I find
all foxes are gifts; afire, already skittering
away at your presence.

2.
Exactness of the inexact
light on Moelwyn Fach;
dusty red-gold of an old
fox.

3.
Every tale is a tale
of parting; the poet's
wife saw through
the kitchen window
a fox fleeing the hunt,
and opened a door
to it. It cooled its paws
in the slate-floored dairy
then left as it had come,
returned to its earth,
tail stiff, a brush
with death.

4.
It pleased you most
to use the word *unruly*,
as you lifted my hair
again from you face,
and rose to make
the coffee.

5.
After the Welsh of Williams Parry

Then with no
haste, no
fright, it slipped
its russet hide
over the ridge.
It happened:
the disturbance
of a shooting
star.

Shevaun Cooley

Five Threnodies for Maralinga:
Part III

When they came to Juldil Kapi,
called Juldi, called Ooldea Soak,
the United Aborigines Mission,
in Jeeps and covered trucks
they looked like moon men.

Soldiers everywhere,
the older ladies recalled.
Guns. We all cry, cry, cryin'.

Time enough to pack a dilly bag
of clothes, a framed photograph,
a child's favorite toy,
before the trucks rolled out,
leaving mission buildings to heat
and swallowing dunes.

And she, between soldiers,
on those hard troopie seats,
secretly fingers a stone
held deep in the pockets of her skirt—
nulu stone, she thinks, last fragment
of the meteor.
Its dust colors her skin.

A hundred kilometers to the south
departing helicopters drop leafets
written in English
warning Aboriginal people
to not walk north.

But here on the savannah,
groups of figures separate in spinifex.

And later, when sky pressed toward them
like a wall, they laid their bodies
over their children
and rose again coated in tar.

Soldiers found them sleeping
in the Marcoo bomb crater.
They gave them showers
and scrubbed their fingernails.
But in the months that followed

their women gave birth
              to dead babies, to babies
              without lungs, babies without eyes,

and their men speared kangaroos
they couldn't cook
because they were yellow inside.

Judith Crispin

Reservoir

Sleeping in its brick tabernacle
the still water is like an ear or radar dish
attuned to distant pulse. Incurious,
we've walked forever to school and work
past locked gates. The saw tooth roof
gives nothing away but scission with sky
and though the key-hole draws the eye, the pupil
contracts. Inside, a herringbone of oak beams
and rafters hovers over the water's weight
and repose. Beyond the inscrutable iron fence
the street's steep uphill/downhill zeal;
urban windows; the domestic race
of breakfast, phones and life and birth and death.
Inside this null-and-void this leave-no-trace
the morning sun has picked the lock,
entering through a gable's little porthole,
bending light with its oblique know-how.

Sarah Day

I Saw the Devil in the Cane Fields

in the Atherton summer.
My nose was bleeding and there
was no one out, not for miles or months.
        My father
had followed the lake boats to Eyre.
He used to tie Jitterbees
to Eagle Claws, and name the bait
after my mother. But
he never caught anything,
not for years, so he named the bait
after me instead.

The devil held my hair back
as I washed my face in the kitchen sink.
The air was sticky and I could taste
ozone in the back of my throat.
        The other boys
had found scorch marks
in the western fields, and my hands
still smelled of burnt sugar.
The devil and I sat at opposite ends
of the tiny dining table and listened to the roaches
scuttle beneath the refrigerator.

I watched the devil take the east road,
hands in pockets, eyes on the stars.
        His shadow
kept me company in the door
frame. One day's walk to reach Cairns.
He had a sprawling gait
and I thought, perhaps next time,
we'd try dancing.

Shastra Deo

Barnacle

I cut myself on a four hundred
year old barnacle. It was my fault.
I strayed into its seaside territory
by mistake. The ocean ambushed
me in the beach's narrowed alley.
Cursed in a language before blue.
Its wine-dark shoulder-charge
knocked me onto its cobblestoned
street; my hand parachuted open,
launching like a grappling hook, but
gravity hid behind my legs & pulled.

Its edge opened up my palm neat
as a pay envelope's promise. It
was part of a razor gang after all,
its cutthroat mates flashed shivs too.
Hard to imagine their cave hideout,
a distant cousin to the Himalayas was
once a mass of lifeless sea creatures;
fishbones, bleached coral, mother
of pearl, shell, grit rasped into smooth
particles by the tide's kinetic sawmill
& risen as mountainous tomb.

Darwin studied them. Rubbed his
stiff fingers over their stars, old as an
Elizabethan dirk. He knew an organism
that lived so long, must know something
about morphology, longevity. Measured
their jagged coastlines, counted bubbles
that escaped from their miniature craters
He cut himself too, proffering his own

blood for science's spell. His revelation.
The simplest live longest, the complex
die sooner from too many moving parts.

Anyhow, my hand opened its red smile,
& rebirthed its salt back into the mother
country's briny womb. My blood oozed
in hot waves, as the flap of skin undulated
like a polyp helpless in a strong undersea
current. This stigmata; blessed ultramarine
pain as though light itself filleted my flesh,
each beam a butcher's knife. That was then.
The scar is bone white as the string of dead
coral & cuttlefish backbone left by a high tide.
My children's children's children will see it die.

B. R. Dionysius

The Throne

In crisis
I go to the local library
and do not take out
the book I find,
this one or that one first,
what matter?
Outside beside my car
sits a strange chrome and vinyl seat,
part of a vanity set,
stranded, hieratic, ruined,
like the beautiful straight-backed
low seated chair-people
of Saint Martin d'Ardèche.
I do the visual maths.
Will it fit behind?
—no, there, rightfully, is the seat for our grandson—
I consign its odd allure to my phone's photo bank instead.
I sit on it only once,
open its cream frayed seat
with its tooled insignia of promise
—*nothing*—
What does it mean
for home to be a failure?
What does it mean
for other places to be a failure?
I leave the throne to its own
mise en scène, neither
desolate nor replete
were I to claim it.
There is, after all, no mirror
in front of which to place it
though I fix my hair and do my lips
before I reverse away.

Lucy Dougan

Six Afterimages

Peter Lanyon

those quadrilaterals,
hedges, a landing strip
seen through cross-hairs

that line, a strut or cliff edge
a sudden dip or buffet
a broad slash of blue

landscape, suggested once by a Claude glass
might be just this... this... this,
like ornithology: 'for the birds'

Frank Auerbach

down Primrose Hill
two lights, feeble in middle ground,
hemmed in by shrubbery

orange visibility vests on a lime coloured oval
a street wet behind glass
pedestrians lit by the glow of phones

the open cigarette packet on the pub table
is a strategy, pencil backwards
on the interlocutor's ear

dusty window panes
haloed by sunlight
bright squares on a bar floor

Alexander Calder

ballet shoes point upward
a slight figure, lifted

by a thickset one
the weight of both

an absence, suggested
by continuous line

so the testes become a leg
an elbow becomes a signature

the space enclosed
animate;

across the aisle
Josephine Baker

dances, her shadow
lifeless on the wall

Gustave Courbet

The cliffs of Ornans appear
as they do through the gallery window,

the local characters enlarged, a bourgeois presumption
to be bigger than Napoleon (a short man),

to inhabit a large canvas, as though
worthy of the academy.

What made him present himself, greeted on the road
by another figure (engaged perhaps

in mere commerce?) offer instead of an epithet
a commonplace?

Jacopo Bassano

Light breaks (or fades) over a distant mountain
but the figures in the foreground are too intent

to notice, animals martialled up a ramp in pairs,
eggs collected in a basket. The humans

bundle possessions, sort copper pans, have
no time to view even the rising water.

To the left a monkey holds what looks like
a sceptre – has all sense deserted these people

alive in the cramped space of a jigsaw? All questions
seem to have an answer in this world

but where is the cat's companion?

Basil King

The face could be
lunar, its craters

the glint of an eye,
bend sinister of the mouth;

half is in eclipse,
an orange shadow,

the other half glances out
at invisible events,

history maybe, or
just a present

occurring somewhere
behind you;

a glow, or
halo surrounds it

Laurie Duggan

Distance

After Jordie Albiston's 'Cartography'

What is the space between this hut and that mountain
but impenetrable black, and frosty cold.
She is writing this at a table in the cabin,
spinning thoughts like threads, as if they can hold

her boys tighter, pull the mountain in, with their bold
tents blooming like flowers in the snow.
Can thoughts, or mad desire, shift the world
slightly, tilt ranges so their faces lower

to her own? Upthrust, tectonic forces, the whole slew
of geology sped up, so contour lines diminish
and lakes freeze, ice thickening to a deep blue
while those dark mountain peaks relinquish

distance; and this long night will finish.
Her writing is a thread to lure them back,
their faces filled with snow light, dolerite, the itch
of time alone, the cold breath of height. Face facts:

the contours between here and there are shifting. Pack,
and ask, what is the space between home and out there,
between their beginnings and these beginnings, but a lack
of courage; what is distance but a prayer?

Adrienne Eberhard

The Apology Day breakfast

my mother did not grow up
with her mother I did not
grow up with mine my son
did not grow up with me

how does one define the jigsaw
when the pieces are misshapen
by the constant hands of others?

the gift of life is maternity
and the removal of this is
a reparation that has no price

the picture is askew in the portrait
you offer and rejection is the new
graffiti to rewrite the script

you offer breakfast and forget
I found my mother
and rebirthed my son
Together we are the Banquet

Ali Cobby Eckermann

La Vita Nuova

A flock of them that day took to the sky,
The paragliders, harnessed loose and slung
Precariously to fly
The steppes of air, those empty replicas
Of paddocks, where their shadows warped and swung
Like a windborne attack.
Above them, though, began to magnify
In roiling folds what was
About to take her life, and give it back.

From all that flight of dozens, it plucked her.
A miles-high mass, it snatched her parachute
At the perimeter
And sucked it in, and up the roaring siphon
Of pressure, hail and black light in dispute
To grapple and transform
Her body to a frozen armature,
Which lofted with her life in
Suspension up to the ceiling of the storm.

Almost an hour she hurtled in ascent.
Unconscious soon enough, with eyelids sealed,
She missed the main event:
The luminance, the lightning-ravished caps
Of clouds. The parachute would likewise yield
And, long before the summit,
Froze rigid as it bore her upward, bent
Around her in collapse,
Then, spat out at the top, began to plummet

Down all the storeys it had climbed before,
But now outside the storm. Who could have guessed
That falling would restore
Her life to her and thaw the chute, which snapped
Immediately open to arrest
The plunge where she was bound?
With ever wider swoop and glide it bore,
Incredulous and rapt,
Her cold but breathing body to the ground.

Stephen Edgar

Putting on your boots

The child's boots are tough brown leather with holes
in each side of the heels for the prongs of the callipers.
The callipers themselves have steel rods at the sides
and, at the top, wide leather bands to circle the swell
of the calves. Each band's held tight by buckles
and straps, each fixed with a buckle's thick needle
through one of five eyelets in the strip of the hide.

The skin of my hands is soft and light, faint
with peach. With my young fingers, I ease the boots
onto your feet, pivot the callipers into place, tighten
the straps and, standing behind you like a spine straight
to your curve, hold you close, and with my right foot
nudge your right foot. And when your right foot has slid
forward, with my left I nudge your left.

Together we take three steps until you slacken
in my grasp. Those callipers, you know, were long
gone when you died in the quiet of a private
room. It would be overly romantic to say that you
walked from the world. The night before, we sat
with you, through the seizures and the flash of diodes
spelling oxygen saturation and pulse.

I returned just after you had slackened, your flesh
warm beneath my touch. There was the old scar
on your ribs where a bed sore had formed
like an eyelet in the skin for a needle of normality
and there, too, the persistent curve of spine. You left
us so gracefully with smiles for those who stayed
as if dying was the most natural thing to do just then—

like the way a peach holds and gives its juice
or a calf's skin lends itself to a child's calf
and a child's fingers learn the workings of a thing.

Anne Elvey

Because, like the weather

Because, like the weather it colours this place
you do not notice. Maybe, you'll sense
in the way something is put, something avoided,
neatly, because though they're friendly enough,
no matter how long you have been among them
you can't be trusted to understand. How could you?

      So, I tell this as an anecdote.
They'd been seeing it for some time,
even caught sight of it padding by the back door,
its stink down by the chook pens,
but now it's here, in a cage they'd set
with one of the lambs it has killed.

There is panic in the froth of saliva.
Eyes engorged with brilliance.
      Their dogs, the fox.
They bay and snap at the cage.
It is sweat-matted and concentrates its stare
on its newest threat, swivels and snarls,
and snarls and is lost in the mash of its fate.
      One by one
a new dog is introduced
until terror extinguishes with a yelp.
The cage, silent as the hills,
      as all witness is.
"The best way to blood pups," he says.
Trusting me with that much.

Russell Erwin

The Art of Birds

Golden pheasants

Nature invented art,
so they remind us — gripped by
their need to seed self-
copies ad infinitum:
each one a mobile Venice.

Mallards

with sequined green heads,
cobalt wing-panels, change to
feathery icebergs
while they feed from the depths; rise
with iridescent sang-froid.

Glossy ibis

So eerily red —
a Mephistopheles bird.
Nests deep inside sedge.
Just a hint of Art Deco,
with Egyptian blue-green eggs.

Lady Amherst's Pheasants

True aristocrats —
bodies, solid as trust funds;
each tail, a poised quip.
Head-capes, fanned wide in display,
show them artfully one-eyed.

African Greys

They snub pleasantries,
obsidian eyes agleam —
each glance shrewd, icy.
If revenge were to be had,
what torture would they devise?

Corella

She swoops in, close to
the heads of the audience,
does tricks as required,
talks back with quizzical zest.
Flirty eyes, bright as gumdrops.

Bleeding-heart pigeon

A crimson stab-wound
on its delta of sluiced red —
a living symbol
set off by plumped beige, flinty
grey: the shades of *schadenfreude*.

Greater Bird-of-Paradise

Once, on boughs near clouds,
acrobatic moves all day,
the flounce and flick of
plumes — yellow, airy silver;
many ticks on the dance card.

Azure-winged kookaburra

An old chuckler with
summer skies emblazoning
his wings; the browns of
wattle bark and river dirt:
an uncanny completeness.

Diane Fahey

The Snake

i'm not Building   a House, though i

go Under them   like a Low creek

i'm not Playing   a role when My

de Facto hip   hits the Stage or

bumps the Record   my winding Mind

a human Feeling   a mental Flexing

with a Whiff of dead   bird Or mouse, to

the Discerning. i   head to the Eternal

Verandah, discarding   contortions and Blue

herrings. i Have   a Diamond on my head

some Frost on my tail   and Apple on my fangs

Turning's what counts   the Steady tone, transfixing

people with Ears and   Winters under their

Belts. i drag my   Belly through the dirt

yet am Clean enough   by the Time i enter

the Australian literature   library to Shed

my skin. i'm Always   there always Travelling

shifting Shape, leaving   a Wriggle where it'd

been Said was nothing   or Maybe a trickle

long Dry. did i   say I'm a feeling

a sober Mood   part grim part True?

Without intent   and yet with Business

to Attend to   social Habits to

pursue and Contest   at my Best i

wear a Helmet   and a Nettle dress

perhaps you Saw me   exit the Ocean

from your Eyrie   or Unblessed yacht?

or Felt me enter   your Swimmers while tanning

but That's decades   ago. i was Still

highly Pastoral then   not So forgiving

now I'm ecumenical   the Word of god

or Sod suits me   Seduction itself's

just Education   or lies to Protect

the needy. Rest-   lessness is my Mainstay

the Road as seen   from an Alpine car

or cushioned Chair   Risk need not be

forced. any Minute   Momentum might be

blocked, or Random   disrupted Joying

devolve to Vice   and Spice my life

with Strikes or cut me   Dead, how annoying

Michael Farrell

For Cornflowers to Sing

Blue must be stolen.
There must be purple
plums, cherries, telling us
blue insists on the flower.

The silence of the jar
must be the centre
which grows the painting

Unlatches stillness,
resists composition,
detonates the seasons.

For cornflowers to sing
each line must scar
its making.

There must be light
and the idea of a window.

In each fold of creamy linen,
blue corners
crouching under the table.

For cornflowers to sing
they must be fallen.
Blue slalom.
White grave of the table.

Susan Fealy

'For Cornflowers to Sing' is a response to Brett
Whiteley's *Still Life with Cornflowers*. The title is
an adaptation of 'for the cornflowers / to sing …'
from 'Cornflowers' by Robert Adamson.

Main Street Social

O Hail! to the days of wine and typhus,
the arrangements of battlefields in early spring,
the glory of a factory that rifts your body
before it wipes your mind, religions vivid
as blood sacrifice. Rise up King Pepe!
Pwn the noob descending the staircase,
these Chads will know the beta's far cry.

PTSD was straightforward
when you could just belt your wife.
These days all we have is a toilet stall
where you can sharpie "Ted Bundy
would have loved her as prey"
across a picture of Patricia Krenwinkel
and no one will delete it.

These days it seems to me
people have their favourite monkeys,
bonobos or capuchins, smart as dumb likers.
I might just borrow yours.
Welcome to the shit show
and remember to vote with your wallet.

Liam Ferney

Stones

For Ellen Hinsey

My whole surface is turned toward you,
all my insides turned away.
—Wisława Szymborska, 'Conversation with a Stone'

The pebble
is a perfect creature
—Zbigniew Herbert, 'Pebble'

We generally assume
they've no interior or soul.
When we break them open
they present a new exterior.

They're a fraction more
than nothing: a quality
of hardness, a resistance
to our touch. To our sight

bounded shapes: unmoving
inanimate. We speak of their faces
only metaphorically: lacking eyes
and mouth, at most they're blank.

But sitting by this stream
I'm struck by your simple
presence. Meeting you
the water slows and wrinkles,

rushes on. Not going anywhere
to you it's all the same whether
you're clothed in moss or bare,
dappled, in sun or shade.

The stone is worldless, Heidegger wrote.
But is this a deficiency? I agree
their detachment's perfect;
they seem outside relation—

to call them *you* a conceit—
indifferent to our distinctions:
geologic, metamorphic, igneous
sedimentary, sandstone, true or false.

But this afternoon as I worried
about what to write and do, they
and not the versatile stream,
appeared as sage—in the world

beyond the world, as though
they were primeval Buddhas
who attained complete humility
and sunken in meditation

hardly noticed death—
only an increase in light.

Luke Fischer

27 Materialisations of Sydney Cloud

a tsunami (risen above an east coast low)
a dust red dawn
an electric bluebottle jellyfish
a pleasure cruiser
a head of beer (frothing over glass towers)
a colony of gulls
a pavlova (sunbaking)
an oyster
a mosquito net
a bushfire's black ghost fingers
a soft koala (somewhere above The Rocks)
a haemorrhage
a fancy suit
a low-flying plastic bag (against a screen-blue sky)
an Utzon structure
a blankie for the supermoon
a bank
a vapour trail of bats
a brown Holden (leaded petrol)
a total fucking gas
a purple stucco ceiling spray-painted pink
an undulating sprawl
a giant pomeranian (recently washed) above a park full
       of smaller white fluffy ones
a waft of Turnbull rhetoric
a layer cake of development flats
an asteroid belt
a shark

Toby Fitch

Before the Storm

This afternoon there is a soft knocking at the door, it is the sound that leaves make when they brush against glass. A man is staring at me through the flyscreen. He has the manner of a flight attendant, or a nurse. The sunlight is mussing up his hair, which is grey and thinning but was once a deep black, one imagines. He is sewn over his bones. He knows my name and says it like a prayer that is repeated every morning, upon waking. I reach my hand into the black, damp past and feel about in it, among sightless things that glide on the ocean floor. *Dad?* I ask, but this is not a question. It has been fifty years since I called a man my father. On the windy surface of memory, my mother is tangled in her bed sheets, and the long cry of loss. He reaches his arms towards me, like a man who is fumbling in the dark. *Oh my boy*, he says, *my boy*. We are standing at a threshold, where there are lives to be known, and time lost. The afternoon has tired of itself, collects streetlights. Dusk is shuffling through the undergrowth of houses. A storm is coming over.

John Foulcher

The Western District

My uncles had set that day to do the whole thing,
and the day was forecast to be clear.
That meant locals and their other mates
magnetising to the paddock spot:
a circle of utes and unemployed old wagons
radiating out in degrees of exhaustion:
not much of a word said
for the cold of the march ahead.
The job was: excavating a fair old trench
for burying hay up to its head:
stacking, not bumbling in, the bales:
tarpaulining the whole thing,
a dozen men making a ginormous bed
expertly of the earth:
tucking in the edges with the weight
of immensely heavy, robust tyres
that had to be hiding the apertures
they had in them. Like you ever do
at that age, you attain a little grassed
hillock with an ideal view of things.
By midmorning I had picked my
vicinity of fascinating dirt bone-dry
of daffodils. The trench was then the
beginning of a knee abrasion:
the earth was pushing back with
crevasse-cracks, elastoplast-ied collarbones
of clay. Lunch was a distracted
looking-on, a flinty-eyed imagining
over sandwiches about how and
from what angle to attack things next.
Afternoon was the cruellest month,
and dusk was just unconscious will,

the bit I didn't, and will never get.
The half-light made them all shadows
of hauling, appalling efforts. The last tyre
went down, was met with a spectral
acknowledgement. Not a soul had left
out of fear of abandonment of
any other diarised thing in their lives:
the desire to get it done, however
mental and not ergonomic that was,
was all, by the end.

William Fox

Unkempt if You Will

Unkempt if you will
mazy with grass seed and insects.
By which you read Summer.
A season warm and static. Nothing
surely can happen beyond the buzz
of the bees in the salvia. Stay here, lie
on the lawn the whole day
until its light and heat dissolve into night
until at last we must seek shelter.
Forget about the dog, unpredictable
on the boundary, the strange look
she gets in her eyes as she lunges,
hurls her longing and discontent
repeatedly against the fence.

Angela Gardner

Empirical VII

Storm water piped under the cutting comes out here,
unfolding down under the surface of itself, bluish oil-haze
clotted with seeds and insects—and down the gully
dank onion weed tracks the secret paths of water—Late winter,
black cockatoos scrap and cry in the Monterey pines
which bank the gully's side—The water flows to a standing pool
out the back of the CSL where a metal trap stops leaf-litter and
    bottles
and the massed reeds are that washed-out grey
which shines at dusk—From the wetlands water is pumped
up to the golf course or sometimes floods the creek, now a
    concrete drain
beside the motorway into the city—Across the gully
the factory generator begins itself repeatedly—Behind the
    cyclone fencing
its rooves stack the horizon—Smoke from its furnaces,
    widening out
through shadow like scratching on a lens glass, is suddenly
    there,
lit coils across the brick wall of the factory, blank updraft
    swarming
in and out of light that whitening shiver out the back
of magic lantern slides, invented depths giving its close scenes
    place—
The rain is first a screen that folds in on itself its infinity
    of repetitions, nerve-end flares, and then the leafless furze,
its each thorn strung with unrefracted rain, is the
    infrastructure of a cloud
stopped on the gully's side and at each step vacancy
scatters out of the pale tops of the grasses, untellable, singular,
    immune—

Lisa Gorton

Inheritance

Bigger than Christmas,
the Borroloola Rodeo announces
      itself with a mushrooming of camps
      as show trucks and outstations
chorus below a starlit big dipper
out on the edges of town:

      I unroll my swag
with Buffalos—the Gudanji mob
      from Bauhinia Downs, Cow Lagoon
      and Devil Springs—where this year's mood
is a carousel cracker in acclaim:

at the camp centre
      a 55-gallon drum is suspended
      between the forks of two trees
         by ropes bound
      to their anchor points
      with the neatest of figure-eights;
a mastery of makeshift mechanical bull:

      out on the edges
the kids practice their hondas,
      an overhand knot with a stopper
      at the end threaded through
and tightened down
      to form a nearly-perfect halo,
the lasso is a dream flung
               bang-on:

throughout our camp
tarpaulins hover like magic carpets

giving shade and privacy
as ropes and uprights are fastened
                    with rolling hitches—
a season's banked domestic security:

and this year our ropes lash
                    together such calm relief
        in the managed risk of a rodeo's spills:

        this year we are spared
the dawn drop and swing
when the rope is laid down
                    in a wide sideways "S",
        the end wrapped round thirteen
times to form a loop tightened
for the end:

this year
        when dawn breaks
the bull rider's eight second rattle
                    is our only breathless
                                yield.

Phillip Hall

Heart's Core Lament

The lawless manner in which these sealing gangs are ranging about requires some immediate measures to control them. From what I have learnt and witnessed, they are a complete set of pirates going from island to island along the southern coast, making occasional descents on the mainland and carrying off by force native women.
—Major E. Lockyer, 1827.

The parents are great hindrances to the improvement of the children, and will continue to be so for several generations unless some decisive measures are adopted, to separate in a degree, the one from the other.
—M. Moorhouse, Protector, 1842.

The mission stations are doing a good work, for if the natives under their influence were not taken care of they might wander about, getting into mischief, and put the country to great expense... The half-castes are more intelligent than the pure-bloods, but they cannot reasonably be expected to come up to the standard of whites.
—M. Hamilton, Protector, 1903.

Charlotte   oh Charlotte   on whaling ship we came   seized jewel-harbor country   from Albany enslaved   they harpooned rugged coastlines   their chase was for the pull   bound east-ward South Australia   your body wretched under rule   lamented life   my Charlotte   you fade without a trace   a whaler's flesh-trade cargo   your terror   our cold-case

he was stolen to Poonindie   blessed to tame   subjugate   all Bible-versed   body-cursed   Reverend's call to educate   Protector-issued rations   the boy was trained to count and save   oppression reigned with daily bread   yet learned he became toiled wide-brown-land beyond his class   then forced to move away

steamers glide to Coorong's heart   Taplin's Mission Point McLeay   vast glistening lakes   weaving-reeds   frame homes of stone and clay   in nineteen-0-three I was born   to my gentle mother's hand   as Superintendents penned Protectors   surveillance-file demands   forced on steamer once again   displaced now three-times from my lands

Point Pearce Mission Station   our strong grandmothers are born   against blood-red far horizons   against white-crosses as they mourn   they rise with eyes cast hard and low church-bells toll a strict routine controlled confined objectified   starved punitive regime   petitions signed by all our men   demand conditions to improve   for blankets to warm our Old-Ones   for young girls lost to servitude

I could do more with them if obedience was enforced; but as it is the parents interfere so much… There is such a demand for them as raw material. They can all wash dishes and scrub floors.
—Royal Commission on the Aborigines, 1913.

she serves her bluestone-master   she falls tragic to the moon   she hangs her apron-sorrow   every hot-gold-hush of noon   he sets her place at meal times   with dogs on cold-stone floors   he throws a bone   nods his head   makes her beg for more   'I couldn't bear the kitchen work'   by misconduct I abscond   I run for rugged ranges   to shadow winds   where I belong

this drought won't break
this drought won't break

…as native citizens of this country we claim the right to have been consulted before any measure dealing with our children in this way was brought before parliament.
—E. Chester, Point Pearce, 1921.

this drought won't break   my country   under pitiless blue sky   colonial-amnesia reigns supreme   over stifled ring-barked cry   sick at heart   my country rise-up   dance for rain   trace this blood-land-memory   flooding through our veins   bear witness our shared-history   past-future stories call   core of my heart   my family   spectral imprints shape us all

Natalie Harkin

The Tent

I've had that dream again
of musk and wet

the earth a flower
reaching up beneath sawdust

for the hip bone
that presses closest to the dirt

I would not sleep
if not for the small circle of light

where the pole pushes
through the sky's fabric

and a miniscule glimmer
of moon trickles down

the fabricated wall
            when I was small

I heard the sound of a rabbit
grazing nearby

and a bull hollering on-heat
under the drape of the seasons

I thought of smaller and smaller homes
(burrows cans shells)

because of this I am able
to diminish myself

become a ball a marble
fluff

it's as if
when the noise of the world

overruns the camp
I am safely camouflaged

but it is at night
when clothes

lie fallow
and audiences drift away

I see the soaring dirty lid
of canvas open

and the stars arranged
in a show unparalleled

Jennifer Harrison

Acrocorinth

Time has scalloped and tightly crimped
the hill's stone—all the troughs

and rifts of its flanks studded
with cypress, laurels. The Acrocorinth

juts into wind above the yellowed vineyards
and timber pig-sheds, the fish

like wands of garnet or black-spotted quartz
carving the shallows at Vrahati beach.

My grandfather's people
coaxed

clusters of bitter-and-sweet jade fruit
from the vines, while time—like a god's

hand on the hill—tapped off seams
of limestone with the rain's pick, or pounded out

trenches with fist-fulls of hail, lightning.
In the village, pines drip

resin in the brush. I walk
dirt tracks where hens pace for seed. In dusty

gardens, in olive groves, the goats swank
oily beards, the hammered scrolls

of horns, gnashing thyme thickets - the Acrocorinth
pale as whey to the south. From here

I make out the old acropolis extruding
from the hill like blunted teeth; I probe,

till my eyes ache, for Aphrodite's
temple, nesting somewhere in the high

ridges. The Corinthian Gulf flickers
down a north-east road, and I know

this evening the sun swill strut there like a peacock
trailing long feathers across

the water. Soon, I'll walk back
to my great uncle's house.

He'll empty wine from a barrel.
He'll tell me stories of his brother's fist.

I've seen the x-rays—my mother's
dented wrist, forearm—all the fractured

bones. And I'll think of those hands,
coaxing, on the vines; and I'll think of a god

with a fist-full of hail. I'll drink
the cool, bitter pink liquid, and currents

of sweetness will twist
through each mouthful.

Dimitra Harvey

Zero Degrees

Rags of snow unmelting on the southern lawn.
Those younger ones, whose death turns

on the hair's-breadth incidence of accident,
avoid this perduration of slow misrecognition.

He dreams his cotton blankets are combusting,
but won't press the hospital buzzer because

the nursing staff are occupied extinguishing flames.
That vandals have broken into the cupboard

of the genial stroke victim in the bed next door
who says only, 'Here it is'. That children are being

shorn in the corridors. That a chaotic darkness has fallen
on working class districts erased for the concrete husks

of a hulking and labyrinthine construction: apartments
for immigrants and foreign students, with mirrored windows

replicating glare to the suburban boundaries.
The view is of a miniature city in a bottle of smoke,

car pollution mingling with vaporised frost.
An extended family of currawongs gathers

expectantly for the faintest turn of leaf litter.
He requests that his communist newspapers be hidden

in case they are reported – but doesn't say by whom –
and remembers an article he once wrote for *The Nation*

about poverty in the Blue Mountains: a young mother
with three clenched children, all without jumpers,

the temperature never lifting above zero degrees.
Soon a plush Pullman carriage will arrive to transport him

to the plains for further tests, flashing through all
the usual stations: *Bullaburra, Linden, Warrimoo.*

John Hawke

The Hanged Man

At the time of writing to you
The sun sets over Sydney Harbour
Bizet's *Carmen* bursts out on the water
Full moon rises over the bridge
Valentines clink glasses and part
        Clink glasses and part

In Melbourne a southerly blows across the bay
The mercury drops to thirty
Madame Sosostris sets The Lovers alight
Fireworks explode in the sky
Rainbows spread over the face of the moon
              And rub out the stars

Ropes of rain drop on Esperance
Pods of pilot whales shore up to die on Farewell Spit
Cascading waters bite into America's tallest dam
Everywhere on the planet lakes fill with fish doped on
    antidepressants
Margaret Atwood's *Year of the Flood II* (non-fiction) is released

In Paris refugees huddle together outside the Sacré Coeur where
cleaners slip them Halal baguettes

In London a Tory student films himself burning a £20 in front of a
homeless man

In Manhattan the Statue of Liberty cringes

At the time of writing
George Orwell has just published *Twenty Seventeen* (non-
fiction)

At the time of writing
Maryam Mizakhani dons no Jihab but wins the Nobel Prize for
mathematics

At the time of writing
China prepares for war
North Korea fires missiles into the Sea of Japan
Syria and Afghanistan bury their new dead

At the time of writing
The planet is tilting off its axis
Coal-fired power plants belch
Robotic bees are born

At the time of writing
I want to kill time
Forget all possible endings to the world
Remember the boy who launched off his bike on the gravel way
back when we were immortal

At the time of writing
Death has achieved her majority
Madame Sosostris grants you eternity
I tuck away the Hanged Man's card

Dominique Hecq

Works Cited:
Atwood, M., *The Year of the Flood*, Vintage, Toronto, 2010
Eliot, T. S., *Collected Poems 1909–1962*, Faber & Faber, London, 1963
Orwell, G., *Nineteen Eighty Four*, Penguin, Harmondsworth, 1984

Inchings and Belongings: After Paul Strand

1.
The building's torn down – an irreducible light, a blow to the knee
you received there, flights of literature in stacked paperbacks.
We saw books gather our balcony, glancing from slow pages to
that grimy world. We shook traffic noise from ears. So much
to keep that we couldn't possess, silos of being and memory
suddenly at odds. When a blue-inked notice arrived we stood
in outrage, debating what to do – we would not have our lives
resumed. But we'd no rights in the matter and months absorbed
us in shifting away. On the day of demolition *Thomas Crimmins
Contracting* moved equipment in. Walls fell on our doings; light
flooded damp ground. I saw a paper bird that looked like
one you'd made last Christmas, among rubble. You'd already
walked into the alleyway where the baker had been, riddling
our mornings with yeasty smells. "No," you said. We left dust to
permeate that air and gathered the spectral into our seeing. We
found no further words in the broken morning.

2.
Every morning light gathered us in avenues; each evening we
swam in yellowed glass. Summer pressed us down like someone
fixing a stamp. Regularly we bathed in the dirty sea near the
harbour mouth. We knew love like twitchings of light at the end
of bed frames. We gathered being like those fisherman netting
fat, glistening prawns. The city steamed and glowed, summer
stretching out like a body on a bed. In the morning we saw
ourselves as a photographer might see us. On evenings we were
pale fish swimming and turning.

3.

Roots spilled on dark sand like wild calligraphies. We climbed, slid back, clambered again, grasped the long tendrils. You held on to my ankle and hauled yourself up my leg. Our backs held down sand even as wind gathered it. We scrabbled forwards and upwards, finally within reach of high ground. A pathway and cottage, a broken window allowing us in. Two stones on a bench and a smashed porcelain statue. On the cottage's other side, a cliff face and cleft sandstone. A painted gathering of sheep. We stood above fluctuations among fingers of sun and irascible air.

Paul Hetherington

Mister Lincoln or Camp David

i.m. Fay Zwicky

Cormorants at dusk fly in
Under the life-boat shed at the pier's end.
Each arrives at their end
Of a day's fishing, their beaks
Suddenly open, panicky, necks back
As they gain timber and shadow.

For a second I think
They are choking on air
That they might not get to
Folding their wings peacefully for the night
That they might need more medication
Or somesuch.

Ringing off, I can still hear your voice.
I keep wanting to ring you back.
God knows what we might have chosen
To talk about: the Self and its vicissitudes
I suppose, the poems that confined us
The Crazy Janes that would not.

In this garden, there's a dark red rose
On a tall straight stem. A blunt man would
Just pick it for his friend: and how we cursed
The curse of bluntness. Some of its petals
Are edged with black, from frostbite.
I can tell you now it's either called

Mister Lincoln or Camp David.
But you would know that.
The Camp David is thorny.
Each day, when I take my pick of whatever
I can hear your throaty voice
The old smoke still roiling in it.

Barry Hill

Song not for you

After 'Das Lied des Zwerges' ('The Song of the Dwarf'),
   Rainer Maria Rilke

Crooked blood, stunted hands, cripple,
out of place – uncanny how small
thoughts can be, while I'm incomparable,
only a dwarf because the so-called average
person is taller. You ought
to just walk on by, but don't. Ever thought
how inflated you must look from this

height? When I walk or shop, I'm inspiring,
it seems. *Fantastic to see you getting
out*, you say, imagining waking
up in my body, the courage
you'd need not to kill yourself, stat.
How do you live with that?
That's me wondering back,
distractedly eating (wow!) a sandwich.

In my home, I've made it so I come
face to face with the cupboards and oven, belonging
as we all want it. I sleep in my bed (some-
times alone). At work, my cubicle's longer
and wider than yours. True,
this isn't much of a song –
but then it never was meant for you.

Andy Jackson

Head Wound

The carcinoma left a bullet hole
High on my forehead. It looked like a tap
By a pro hit-man. In fact the killer's role
Was played not by a pistol-toting chap
But by a pretty female whose light touch
Sliced out the blob and pieced a flap of skin
Into the gap. It didn't hurt that much.
When finally the pit was all filled in
A pink *yarmulke* of Elastoplast
Topped off the job. The whole thing happened fast.

The wound, alas, healed slowly, but the heap
Of duct-tape mercifully was replaced
By one neat bandage, though I had to keep
Changing it each second day. I faced
At least three weeks of wearing this square patch
And there were interviews for my new book
Demanding to be done. A tale to match
My rather daring James Bond sort of look
Seemed called for, so I mentioned MI5,
A mild gun battle. I got out alive.

No sooner did the first show go to air,
A dear old lady stopped me in the street
And said I really ought to take more care
In gun fights. I thought her a shambling dunce
But only for a moment. All the fault
Had been mine, for expecting that my smirk
Would flag the gag. Alas, there is a rule:
The straight-faced joke that might work on the page
Is death on TV. I should act my age.

Clive James

Barns in Charlevoix

I like the barns, their air of constancy,
their un-renovated geometry, their wooden deshabille,
that they have high hipped roofs — and windows

set without regard to symmetry — that they are unpainted,
the wood grey or brown with age, with parts that lean in
or out, that some are abandoned but endure, that one

imagines the light inside — diffuse and murky
or the doors opening wide and a sudden shaft
of afternoon pouring like honey into dark tea

and the scent of hay and sweet apples on a high
shelf – the horse and cow smells fading,
old leather bridles, iron parts of farm machines,

sump oil, the ammonia of mice,
rough hessian sacks of chaff and bags
of chicken feed, that time here re-collects itself —

sleeps like Keat's Autumn on the bales — and
does not wake but dreams of waisted frocks,
wide hips, foals, fiddles, harvest suppers.

Carol Jenkins

Greenfield development

The white farmer takes a piece of flat earth to market.
She is no flat earther.
But the land's overcropped, and she's *sotto voce* with the throb
of four generations' profit and loss. Skin cancers profit her brow,
hands, arms and legs; four sons field the catch in her voice,
fence her in so she sells quickly. Her nib bleeds out over the contract,
fine cursive streams going nowhere. Hawkish, a pair of cufflinks
and a pair of wide agate eyes, watch. Fast settlements confuse
attachment, history. *Wadawurrung. Wadawurrung.*
When did her boys begin to look like undertakers? She reaches
for her comb, hands it to her middle-aged youngest, his Adam's apple
a jitterbug combine. He wants the deal more than any of them,
is neat enough (most days) to shake hands with a city future.
Outside, the horizon squints, elongates in the heat.
The blistered ute bonnet, parked beside the agent's new car,
rebukes; yet her father's cataract stare once frightened bailiffs.
After the signing, the phone's off for days. When she sees
her best fields carved up, pink allotment flags blowing in the wind,
she thinks it's some new kind of sow stall.
Then lifestyle's cropless verbs appear as billboard signs.
O bury me under the latte lake, she thinks, looking out
her kitchen window, from a past of minute hands,
good black earth and sponges sunk in the middle.
Next day, billboards truck to the lee of the sales office,
marooned in dirt.
Old ewes with pinprick eyes nudge carpeted heads in puzzlement,
gather by strange rectangles of shade. New-poured slabs,
white as snow, cramp thin soil, portals to nowhere.
She holds her mug tight, holds and breaks,
all the lambing woolly beauty of memory.

A. Frances Johnson

Murray andante

The night fills with Bach
with the clear cold
a gas fire doesn't touch
outside rattle of a skateboard
not gelling with the violin

skateboard guy, I've seen him before
rolls back towards Gilbert Street
the slow movement begins
it's not quite a baroque town
the grids almost classical

but the Bach andante claims it
now the outside softens
again giving access somehow
to measure, of steady streets
lack of blue shadow and a

width of days along with my
steady lostness in a bowl
of clarity, while above my eyes
the green and grey hills
need to stretch my thought

and rain suddenly hits the roof
then stops, quick, all this water
that doesn't go to rivers
that doesn't cease the drought
nor bring me back to

a mind that accompanied me
once through funky allegros
and andantes and other
more humid songs
unlike the passing of trams at

Pirie Street, as lawyers progress
to sandstone courts where
cameras linger, sensations of the local
a city's petty crimes
well, that's cross continental

like the sad river, as even
the blind hours remind me
killed state by state, classical neglect
not even this rain nor
this music allays.

Jill Jones

Almost Pause/ Pareidolia

Narcotics cannot still the tooth
that nibbles at the soul.
—Emily Dickinson

Labile wonder, no rabbit-like fear, sea hares
filling the tide pools with their magenta ink are
flamenco dancers as much as mermaids were

dugongs. All those sailors mistaking the docile
monogamists for sirens. How often we graze
our hulls on rocks of clear vision. Still, we have

to see it with our own eyes, their turning tricks
their light desires, billowing in the space between
landforms, soft folds shape. Forest cockatoos

have entered the city. Baroque ripples in their
wingtips indicating stress. Married to what
we intuit as signatures, this persistent cleavage

A sickle shaped leaf at the base of one remnant tuart
Slow chanted count of the mopoke above our heads
While in camp fire ash, the roughly laid out matrice

of squares on a turtle's back speaks of net. Here a man
quadriplegic, has been taught by his mother to make
a sign of the cross with his tongue. Number

the things played out in the mouth. Language hesitates
to enter the concealed strand of vertebrae beneath
a dark lick of scales, uncoiling across blackened remains

of balga, racing as snake into our shared vision. Our
hands extensors and abductors gripping themselves
riven in resistance, the words 'beyond regeneration'

heard again in a stand of sheoaks. We can follow
the blood red trail of uneaten zamia nuts out
of scalded wetlands. Mining mountains no longer

unmoved, even this verse cannibalizes itself
remembering the feast to come. *Like, when I
use the word 'eternity', when what I mean to say, is 'water'.*

Amanda Joy

To Paint the Inside of a Church

After Tarkovsky's Andrei Rublev

Beneath the glamour of the pipe organ
there are bellows. Underneath the church
of the Grand Prince there's the dour
obligation of immortality
as if it were the family business,
and preparation for an abiding name
exists like Latin classes.

Andrei is trying so hard
not to make a mark or a sound
but cannot help it—something unattached
to ego drives on this faith painting,
though the body that germinates
belief still throws such shade
he feels impelled to the crossroads
of yellow flowers buzzing
so full of bees that if this scene were shaken
upside down it would not be pollen
that trickles out but legs and wings.

Beneath the pipe organ's glamour
there is a pit that breathes
and every tone must be mixed precisely.

Imagine the months and years
of painting the inside of a church
while others have their tongues cut out.

To paint the inside of a Russian church
dome in the fifteenth century
is to be the very sound of a bell.

*

A fire once started can take care of itself—
all it knows is *eat*.
It can clear a field so nicely.
This can be good or bad for us.
No rules call and there is no dialogue
with the conscience,
only giving things to fire and
allowing the instinctive *eat*.

Andrei did not approve of how the pagan
woman loved but I think she won.

To live inside a church
whose walls you paint
is to live a life of scaffolds.
His shroud is a bell.
His cloak is a bell,
feet bells and all the violence

he sees is a tonal gradation
towards the most splendid red—
one forever repeated blow
and its resonance.

Carmen Leigh Keates

On Loss

I

And when I go there now
sometimes at night
the old familiar paths
deserted, and the trees
just stirring in the sky,
I call your name.

The agapanthus are in bloom
death flowers, and the
peach tree looks small
and ordinary now,
but then, that morning
it shimmered in the light
a dream of whiteness
alive and unashamed.

II

So many seasons now
life goes on
unchallenged
unaware of us.

This cut, this total
final cut
like a dead weight
that presses down.

Death needs no one
comes wrapped
in self-sufficiency.
Do you hear?
You all who strive
for self-sufficiency
this is the way.

Antigone Kefala

A New Norcia Subset

The Benedictine community at New Norcia inflicted sexual abuse on school students on an almost unprecedented scale in Australia during the twentieth century. Further, given New Norcia's control, displacement and exploitation of Aboriginal children and people, everything we write about the place has to be viewed in this context. The poem itself cannot exist alone, cannot exist outside this context. This is no longer the grubby secret of the Catholic Church, but public knowledge. No poem can be a celebration.

1. False Starts

Where the great flooded-gum fell or was felled
close to the East Moore River a count of growth-rings
shows almost four-hundred years with guesswork
filling the hollow with logic. And those false starts
where the chainsaw bit and didn't talk, rejected
by a harder layer of time where firebark annealed
against the sawteeth, the vicious chatter, and retreated
then went deeper again to find another rebarbative
layer of history decades ago where something surfaced
in its locale in its heartland, the very essence of its
tree-being its witness of prayers circumferencing
as exoskeleton the language of country reaching
out of its skin to resist and say, We are still omnipresent!
these bites just up from the full cut the absolute
severing from its massive fallen body in segments
alongside a deadend road. This is where we start
and finish, near the blossom-zone of curving grey
honeyeater beaks spiking late-winter nectar making
the seasons name in their system every time they
spark and then chase each other toward progeny,
their sanctifications, their decisive moves
towards a start that will have no end.

2. Cactus Islands in Moore River

Beyond the *forbidden sign* (*heavy machinery*)
where the bridge overs a rapid of a bloated Moore River,
an island either side of the melaleuca-sucking flow—
scum and froth and purity all at once, the grassed
channels conduits for herbicide-orange and malfeasance
of riparian agriculture clotting at the islands' sharp
points and the giant cactuses metastasising the arterial,
the fleshy land. Can we support this image of damage
without it collapsing into metaphor of xenophobia
or can we go back to the dispossessed and claim
on their behalf or are both pictures in a dialogue
through which we might make some sense? Or words
fail when the river flows and when it dries and pools
fester with lunulae of algae and choked microfauna?
I would wonder this and write it differently,
but the mess of thought is pinned to the picture
of where I was, what I take away with me,
what I will return to again: terrorzone to rearrange
in this daguerreotype brain of mine. I am saying
that the spread of cactus *is* a risk to native flora and that we
might extrapolate to make images and analogies
but it doesn't work in this overburdened tableaux
of land and machinery, of newcomers and the less recently
arrived and the people with the oldest claims. They are
all people and as such are celebrated in my ethics,
but I know the science and I know analogies fail
and the literary cannot always be extricated from science
and vice versa and sometimes people wherever
they walk from walk outside the constructs of language,
the semiotics of waking and sleeping and being intact
where you are. The eucalypts are in blossom
and form a fragrant pomander in the box of my head,
extracted by my nostrils. A messy and unpleasant

image, no doubt, but explaining much that adjoins
without annexing my river moment, split between
two Cactus Islands, but cactus islands of glorious
melaleucas and towering, imposing cactuses,
disturbing the balance in a disturbed realm.

3. Reading in St Gertrude's Chapel

In the bivalve half, inner cup
of sound of our own voices where
we are watched over by painted visions.
Outside, visitors search for relationship
to anomaly and for contemplative answers.
This decommissioned girls' school embraces
the terror of secrets, of communion
with cool but sometimes deadly stone—
bricks and mortar, the tendrils of creed
reaching through from the other side of the earth,
passing through the core and igniting futures
outside the enclave. And now, a dozen monks
walk the grounds reciting Dante for next
weekend's performance of the *Inferno*,
from which they'd hope to be safe,
but never gloating as the piano
will play tunes of Gershwin
in variation. But that's a few hours
in the future and due to take place in another room,
at right angles to this room of prayer, with more
external light and a raised stage
where notes might parse without a cross,
without our Lady reading the score
over a shoulder. Listen, between words,
hear her troubled breathing.

John Kinsella

Windborne Avenue

1

There are moths that cross a continent to die in this city.
As black cutworms they suckle Queensland's
saplings but by spring
the heat is already too much and they make the difficult
    passage, flying
by night on an inner compass that draws them
here—a place where nothing is too much, where

shunting down the slender reaches of William Hovel Drive
I forget that I'm alive. A city is
a claustrophobic way to be alone.

Some afternoons I feel the whole city on heat—
the pent-up quarter-ache
in Barranugli's confinements. Though I
love the smell of water simmering in the evening
in a hose left out on the lawn.

2

I want to feel the wind on my back
now that I'm back in the peloton trying
to write to the click-a-clack of my spokes to find a
    meter—any—
on the boulevard of this city windborne
with thighs around me pumping like pistons.

When the frost first lifts from the sprigs
the moths arrive. More than once
through ventilation shafts they've entered

the galleries of parliament—a dissenting
mob demanding only a place to breath in a building
far too much like a flag
piercing the hill's rump at the moment of annexation.

Like that they were embalmed
and the house closed two days for renovation.

3

Between your breasts I rest my head
when the black hair of the afternoon malts in ashen clumps
from five-hundred insolvent
wishes for some modest certainties. From here

I see the gradient of a mountain
baptised with a slur
for the remnants of another people
who dwelt there in the circuit of their own certainties
for durations that can only seem now dreamlike in their
    expanse—
here they gathered to eat moths that chose this place

to die. Let me be like them—these moths—these dizzy
vagrants, churning through the elements on wings
of paper, so fixed on their final coupling
they cannot eat.

Louis Klee

The Corpse Flower Sketch

For John Berger

Sunset, climate-warmed and volcanic –
in the hot sky
a giggle and crake of fruit bats
flown south from development
print themselves in the old money trees
of spooked Park Terrace mansions –
the corpse flower is blooming tonight.

In the Botanic gardens queues
strobed with mobile phone flashes
shuffle under the captive palms
and Titan Arum releases its smell;
part dog bone, part teenage sweat shoe.
A velvety, visceral purple,
pleated curtain around a creamy phallic spike.

John Berger died today in outer Paris;
two more species disappeared somewhere in the world.
After sketching this flower
I will go home and read his *Photocopies* again,
his portraits of ingenious non-celebrity.
Which reminds me it was here, in this opera house
of tropical plants, I last saw my aunt alive.

She who had been a secretary for Menzies
kept her secrets,
but at lunch told us
when she worked for the Southern Cross Hotel
the manager got her to cut up the bed-sheets
the Beatles slept in
so he could sell little squares to the fans.

We came up this walkway
which goes over the lotus pond
and met a bird, a kingfisher flown from who knows where.
Stopping her there in her ninetieth year,
smiling at its magical quality.
Not a word, but a life, and no more than that.
The crowded forest grows inside now.

Mike Ladd

A Tasting

In a bathtub filled with ice I arrange a selection of beers.
Many are from a time when bars were filled
with smoke and blue singlets, others gleam like pilgrims
preserved by winter burial. Some were boutiqued

to the point of being so far up the brewer's coil
distil has been replaced by *crafted* and *essential oil*
as if the word *beer* itself had become linguistically distasteful.
When I open, prematurely, a friend's attempt at stout

flipping the wire swing-arm to release a ceramic cap
a sound like the compressed report of an air rifle
is followed by the reek of creek water, the remains
of dogs, and the hessian bags they were drowned in.

I'm no coinosseur, but I can tell a mongrel
from some hopped-up, spring-fed pilsener
in a cafe-brewery, its blackboard advertising pulled pork
in chalked cursive, the staff drawing beers to Bon Iver

and extolling the virtues of slow food, clean air.
Next I turn to the long necks - favourite of shearers.
For years they were lifted throat-first from fridges
in outstation sheds, opened with a knuckled flourish

and swallowed hard, each bottle tipped over - dead
and dying soldiers on the boards. I can hear the drone
of flies and stories, shorn wethers standing in waves
of lanolin heat, the sun going down like the lid

of a tin knocked from the sky by a .410 shotgun.
Digging, I find a bottle whose label had slipped away
prompting a blind tasting. There is blood, sweat
and the cold residue of a kiss that took me years

to disengage from. Distracted, I keep drinking
craving that one marker for a time when love
was a spell you surrendered to, then passed out under.
Late at night or early in the morning, unable to tell

Melbourne bitter from something a Belgian monk
might have finessed from cuttlefish ink, herbs
and horse blood, I sleep. Waking to a hangover
like contained scrub-fire behind my eyes, the ice

gone to water, the brewing history of five states
and a few home-grown failures competing for space
in my mouth, I lie back and listen to the bells
of the last bottles knocking against each other.

Anthony Lawrence

Zeitgeist

We admire it because it disdains to destroy us:
beauty is nothing but the beginning of terror

Chagall's falling man, a grandfather clock, a yellow
cow with a blue violin populate an allegory of terror

'To punish the oppressors of humanity is clemency;
to forgive is cruelty,' said *le Père de la Grande Terreur*

And an angel of the Lord stood by them, the glory
of the Lord shone round, and they were bathed in terror

Spiders the size of bears, the waking dead, the lights
go out, something claws your arm: the terror

He was a wrist-twister, shin-kicker, a gifted smasher
of cherished things, Verlaine's pale-eyed holy terror

Dear Mr Speaker: I hereby designate all funding for
Overseas Contingency Operations/Global War on Terror

He burns yet doesn't flinch a muscle, doesn't utter
a sound, unlike those who wail and circle him in terror

O say can you see by the rockets' red glare and the bombs
bursting in air the cowardly stern of the HMS *Terror*

Late morning in a climate-controlled trailer a pilot
yawns, scratches his head, and resumes his armchair terror

And an angel of the sword stands by me, the glory
of the force shines round, and I am bathed in terror

Bronwyn Lea

Over the River Memory

Prince Alfred Bridge Gunagagi

When I come back I remember it has
been a long time.
Long time passing since
I came back along this track to Gundagai –
town of my childhood.
There are many ghosts – I hear
their voices.

I stand on a solid red-gum bridge – the
longest wooden bridge in the world.
The Irish nuns told me this on a good
day under the gothic arches in the convent
on the hill where I learnt about Australian history.
'*This continent, Australia, is a young country,*'
they told us. '*The history of this place is very
short – shortest in the world!*'
They'd seen the world – the nuns.
Maps were pinned on the wall to show
how far they'd travelled to spread the word.
I'd only seen my Country.
The longest bridge and the shortest history –
that's what I learnt.

Prince Alfred Bridge they called it – built
last century – by the pioneers as
they opened up the lands for progress.
Our teachers said so.
How many river-gums were felled? What
were their names before they were rearranged
across the river – once their life blood.
What was their history?

My Grandmother said this place is old.
She said my teachers don't know the stories.
I listened.
On a bad day you could be beaten
for asking the wrong questions about
the short history and the long bridge.
At school I learnt to hold my tongue.

The water under the bridge ripples over
my memory now. The bend of the
Murrumbidgee – a deep archive –
flows steady and slow.
I walk on the bridge and I remember how
long it used to take to cross on my little
legs clinging tight to the side rail as huge
wheat and wool trucks thundered over the
ancient planks laden with the wealth
of the nation.

Sometimes the river rose so high it swallowed
the bridge and the town. Short history almost
washed away by higher, older tides.
No trucks now. The bridge long ago closed –
steel and concrete girders bypass the town.
The wealth of the nation rumbles down
different roads.

On the other side I look back across
the flood plains. The old stone convent on
the hill is empty.
I come back after seeing the world.
I hear my Grandmother again.
The bridge is short now.
The history of place – still
long and deep.

Jeanine Leane

Rattling the Forms

I wanted to dissolve my marriage, explode the limits,
seek comfort, oblivion, anything in caves,
on a whaling ship, in a hundred other places.

Shrewd reverie in my perilous head,
I struck out through the shambling waves:
I wanted to dissolve my marriage, explode the limits!

Beyond waterfalls and time lost and the first chastities to mar
    the shore,
defenceless men set me aflame,
on a whaling ship, in a hundred other places.

Not me at all, but my double, my look-alike;
not someone, but anyone in a sort of cloak and hood ...
I wanted to dissolve my marriage, explode the limits.

How bare the narrative seems!
And nothing! And nothing and nothing and nothing ...
on a whaling ship, in a hundred other places.

If you could only see me riding on and on,
babbling like a saint in the open fields!
I wanted to dissolve my marriage, explode the limits,
on a whaling ship, in a hundred other places.

Emma Lew

In Memoriam

On a frosty night,
I quoted Piet Mondrian:
the light is coming.
The trees intoned *it sure is.*

The Great Ocean Road.

Bring closer the wine,
bring closer the moon;
or a spell to forget you,
as the sayings go.

Cassie Lewis

The Novelist Elena Ferrante

I had in my mind cries, crude family acts of violence I had witnessed
  as a child, domestic objects.
—Elena Ferrante

For instance, in Ischia. Those dark corners where the sound does not. But I remembered them that way and only that way do they appear. In each retelling, in the manner of chiaroscuro: stones shearing off the roofs of houses at sundown. Hunting the particularity, the moment, seen so closely from afar. Down the lanes, always in the company of a shadow, a woman, a cleaver. Always closer than before. These slow dances from doorway to doorway—these particular doorways, these particular lanes. My sister—a girl then—clear, cleaving to the shadows, and once. Once we ran from house to house in the dark, calling names, falling and our knees grazed. Dresses stained. Those stones at sundown. Later, in the living room, crowding into corners, watching the walls shake—yellow paper peeling slowly, vertically, folding down in great, wide strips. These days and nights of blood. Clear voices, and distinct, the taste of something metallic. In the corner the broken lamp. The television (silent) in the background.

Bella Li

Epigraph from Elena Ferrante, 'Art of Fiction No. 228', interview with
Elena Ferrante, by Sandro and Sandra Ferri, *The Paris Review*, Number 212
(Spring 2015).

Metronome

Listening to Vladimir Miller sing in
his bass huge as Lake Baikal the song
by Basner about the metronome
on the radio throughout the long
siege of Leningrad, it starts to seem
to me that metronomes tend to lean
to a pattern of two beats then some
small silence rather than a drum
of continuous ticking, even the one
copied with such deathly tones
in the song itself. Binary metre belongs
to life's basic history, alone
reassuring continuity: the poem
or the electronic language on
the internetted brain, the same
tune remains although only one
and a city of ghosts can listen.
The pulse against austerity ticks home
through the blood at the heart of reason.

Jennifer Maiden

Fisheries Raid

Two-face deckies embedded at the caravan park. A month long
operation comes to a head on a Saturday with almost sirens
and headlights. They check each freezer for bodies or just
severed legs frozen into twig piles. All the ballasts are opened
on the boats. All the cars' trunks popped. Who the fuck do
youse think you are, loud across the town. If there's something
in a car it's towed, if there's one too many on a boat it's
dry-docked. Everywhere the sound of phones as neighbours
check neighbours for loss. $25k at number 30, 5k at 24.
Somehow 12 has escaped with a slap on the wrist. Something
not right there mate. Even Skinny trading hobby cray for
tinnies been handed $500 and had his license taken. That's
what it's come to? A mate can't help a mate out. Since the raid
it's only them by the jetty been making any money. Pricks. I
wouldn't want to stay in town tonight if I were them. Wouldn't
want to wake up to a shotto through the windscreen. And
where would they stay, anyway, the motel? Something not right
there. That bloke he's a creep. That bloke can't even thread a
line in no wind and what'll happen now there's nothing left,
I'm done, we're all done in, can't even get the dollars for petrol
to get out of town.

Caitlin Maling

One Way or Another

They can't give you a date
for your bypass operation.
Before Christmas,
if you are lucky.

'We'll be in touch
each Wednesday
to let you know
one way or another.'

And so your future
waits, somewhere
outside, while you
sit inside and re-read

Muriel Spark: *The Takeover,*
Territorial Rights,
The Driver's Seat.
You read them obsessively

each night, as insects
swarm under street lights,
free of consciousness
and futurity.

You see in the New Year,
and time passes,
your nervous system
a shivering horse within you.

But everything can wait,
one way or another,
as you discovered in earlier
visits to the cardiology ward.

The 'code blue' announcements
and even the arrival of
ambulances at A and E
downstairs were less rushed,

more stately, than you
would ever have expected.
Just like the helicopter
outside your ward

those times—lifting off
into the night air,
heavy, and unhurried,
towards some unseen future.

David McCooey

Remembering Sandstone Country

The road is long, always bending
winding through & over sandstone country
a snaking strip of graphite coloured bitumen
pocked with potholes you try to miss
keeping inside double yellow lines
hairpin bends that twist one way, then another
through dark rainforest gullies
small stands of ghost gums & tree ferns
echoing bellbirds, perhaps a lyre bird
then just as quickly drive up along a straight cutting
by the gravel verge, broken bottles, plastic bags
scribbly boronia & wattle, gymea lilies
tall & weathered by the dry, then out onto the ridge
in a blast of sunlight, the sky
                        on a long
sweeping corner we pulled up
at a lookout facing west. We stepped out
into cold wind buffeting, springing from the tops
of a sea of eucalypts, the sweetness of brown boronia
thrown like the scent of light
like electric wild honey in the air
as we walked to the fence & looked out
across a million acres of sandstone country
low flat olive green & blue outcrops
of bleached yellow, orange & grey stone in layers
carved to a rounded valley, eroded by occasional rain, wind
& the endless light of the sun, moon & stars
                                falling
for a few hundred million years in a mist of endlessly
streaming photons, the sandstone
gradually printed in a negative of the known universe.

It's all we saw, the known universe
& all we failed to know, or failed to feel.
A wallaby crashed in the bush below
the universe changed again.

Peter Minter

The Spanish Revelation

Your education came too early, before you had seen an alcazaba
Before you learned about the journey of pomegranates.
You didn't know how to create paradise in a white city
Or the sudden turns these strongholds would have to make
Not to admit your enemies into a garden of oranges
Where the women sit, not quite prisoners,
Gazing through lattices at the bareheaded hills of Spain.

You didn't understand the way God moved through history
Northward with the hacking sword
Revealed through a tribal touch for flowers.
You couldn't allow exactitude and softness to make love
And birth a Caliphate, azure and unflinching
Arches holding up the heart like an eternal Córdoba.
You knew nothing of the interior architecture of your own first name.

In the dark night you smuggled your selves
Out of Tehran, legally or illegally.
Black crows strode down the streets in pairs
Tented, your own small gender, with mystery under the skirt.
On the plane you tugged at your mother's headscarf:
You don't need to wear that anymore.
You carry the girlchild's instinct, you spit in the face of the caul.

Then you found Andalusia and through the hand glimpsed
The divine romance worn by wind and the human palimpsest,
The taste man has for vanquishing himself.
Under the lights of another Roman theatre, lit below the fort
Loyalty grew in mathematics, worship in the stone.
What was past carved itself a resting-place where you could briefly see
Further than a veil, into Revelation, exhaling with the fall.

Marjon Mossammaparast

Anna Karenina

As the train's breath scoops her up,
she remembers Vronsky's boots stamping
outside her door, but also how he delicately
crossed his legs to pull on a new glove.
Hard to judge the gravity of such a gesture
among vile travellers on a muddy platform,
their *sotto voce* spilling out like spiders.
And Alexei's high-pitched voice as he shook
the sweaty hand of Count Bezzubov,
the knock-kneed clairvoyant
who in his sleep could see no divorce.

She judges the two wheels exactly
as if preparing to go into water
for a swim.

No longer the weight of his vanity,
the hooks that dangle in aquamarine rooms
where count and countess
purr the etiquette of butchers.
Now she desires to drift like smoke,
to float over Levin's farm
with its snorting horses and fine fat cattle,
above the poisonous salons of Moscow
and soldiers in strawberry columns,
then come to ground in a choir of wheat
having willed all this at last
with a man's casual hindsight.

Philip Neilsen

Bombala

From the road you see it still,
vanishing in yellow grass,
the old Bombala line—

small embankments, minor cuttings,
low structures over creeks.
For thirty years these pale Merinos

have paid it no attention.
You stop the car, remembering
the signs they had at Central,

those wooden slats with destinations.
Bombala? Where was that exactly?
You contemplate the proud advances:

Cooma, 1889;
Nimmitabel in 1912
(in time for WWI recruits

laughing from receding windows);
Bombala, 1921.
You think too of the politicians

paunched and praising the Monaro,
those conscientious clerks all day
with maps and manifests,

the Chief Commissioner of Railways,
the calm men with theodolites
setting out directions,

the sweaty men with heavy arms
who tap the lines down tight. You see
the first train, rich with dignitaries

and self-congratulation,
the handshakes at the station,
the women standing back a bit

but welcoming the Future. You hear
the soot, the smoke, the hiss of steam,
the driver hooting at a crossing.

The rails are long-since pilfered but
an underlay of stones
and slump of timber bridges still

retain the sounds for those
who care to stop and listen.
It's been just thirty years.

The villages are mainly
growing sleepier.
The bitumen's a winner as

we should have always known.
The price of wool is less than half
of what it was in '53.

Obliging trucks are quick to haul
direct from yards to abattoir.
You stand there in a gap of silence

between successive cars.
You're looking for a word—say *hubris*—
but that is too dramatic for

these blonde and treeless landscapes,
these human traces, half-erased,
surfacing and sinking back

across a narrative of paddocks.

Geoff Page

The Hidden Side to Love

All summer, the bees worked
between bells of laburnum

sockets of foxglove, blades of lavender
—they saw a task and rose to it.

I busy myself with the washing
untwisting funnels of sock, boughs of jumper

rosettes of flannel.

In spare moments I put words in the freezer
reheat coffee, fill inkwells

I stir out hot dinners.

Passing along the hall sheaved in light
I imagine a nectarous meadow

I think of waxen wings brought thudding
to the ground.

I look down at my dress and see spikes of burdock
thistles in plaits hanging all around.

Crayons, soldiers, ropes of daisy
the couch, the doorknob, the stairs—

They all gather to me

Until I stand and rub my hind legs emphatically
until I disengage everything

to its proper place
and emerge like a queen

made anew from decades of trying.

Claire Potter

Pigeons of the Dome

From here on the balcony we see them: pigeons
in Hagia Sophia. They roost high in the dome,
their view is ages old of pilgrims and tourists
crowding the marble floors of this cathedral, mosque,
and now museum.
                        Always they have flown here,
in this still air once hallowed and now profane.
They look down today on these flashlight tourists
as they did on desecrating crusaders whose pirate king
lies buried here, he whose holy marauding
brought him down at last;
                        and then Mohammedans,
sons of the Prophet, spreading the word by the sword.

The pigeons have seen it all. They nest in the dome
as they have from its first raising up, their feathered kind
has prospered two thousand years while kingdoms
have come and gone.
                        They glide in the still air,
while far below, a child looks up from between
her parent and cries for birds trapped, it seems,
as they drift from icon to icon in artificial light
under the arching heavens.
                        Her father, learnéd, devout,
but ignorant of the pigeons' history, murmurs to her,
Aren't we all. Who knows if the arc of heaven will hold?
When the temple falls at last, these birds will surely escape
the cupola, will fly free under the blue dome of the sky.

Ron Pretty

The Lowlands of Moyne

Mud darkening the stories
what's passed down

utterances, quips
a way of looking at fences

the dark stretches
a scattering of bricks where a dairy was.

Farmhouses facing narrow back roads
wrecks of Commodores dumped in cape weed

beside rusted sheds. Heavy country you could
fatten a bullock with. A mother into farm politics

and the boot-deep mud around her dairy.

There were three brothers who drank day and night
until they killed themselves.

A mother who burned her house down
before leaving her husband.

A house with a green roof
fifteen kids came out of.

Children walking barefoot through John's Bush
stealing fruit from Faulkner's fence

after getting the cuts in a one-teacher school.

Stories the paddocks give up
like bits of pipe, old whiskey bottles.

Stories that go right back there
to a baby being brought home in a fruit box

a boy cutting thistles for one and six,
a girl walking away from the smell of onions

to a rail canteen at Spencer Street.

Once a week a draught horse pulls a car by rope
 through water-logged paddocks.

A family of thirteen
cramped and grinning before Mass

slide around behind the horse
hauling them out of their rain-soaked bog.

In the days before electricity arrived
my father said it was like skiing in mud.

Brendan Ryan

Muzzled Altar

The planned onslaught, reedy, timed out with your passage
to starry boulevards
apropos here, winched as caution

Train pocks the country's shore
that shelters behind its painting, or reveals it
as money buttons a screen's
pressing submission or oft-repeated flighty tangent
Alter later
A trophy rolls over the parquet

It was the sliding person not the poem's entrance
as if effusions writ
(on the up, was the combed narrator)
Some wished to rub the shine
petalling beyond itself
Childish sparks reverently fizzle

Gig Ryan

Homeschooling

Because the old
microscope when

we dusted it off was
crudely broken

and a new and subtler one
is coming, we prepare

by rehearsing
rules for handling:

sidelong eye for
precision in lowering

lenses, not headlong;
patience in making

and working slides,
letting cover-slip

drop deftly with tooth-
pick (all these nice

distinctions painful, still
utterly abstract, a prep

for no lab but this
inescapable partnership

from which you'll develop
self-reliant experiment)

and only ever carrying
the weighty instrument

with one hand under,
like lifting a baby

I say, *the way I
lifted you*, and mimic

with empty air now
the shape we made

Tracy Ryan

Strange Music

Mahler's 2nd (The Resurrection) and the Ants

Behind the notes' invisible drama is God. Hearing Mahler
as if lunatics and gravity and ants ceaseless as the first
and second movements the strings and pregnant loads
of differing directions, of front and side and pivoting
chords, or ants unable one at a time to stand still.

Ants as *tendency*, ants as ants in columns on grooves
like dots on CDs the focal movement irrelevant the Sign
and crotchety anywhere of their purpose, their restless
mania for abstraction. No programme notes to read but
then what do Mahler's say — *why do you live? Is it all
a huge joke?* they carry sawn-through leaves as big as
key-signatures, sugar to the living (they rise again) (and again).
No falling back for a cigarette a quick snort a sinus moment
of whisky or cocaine just to keep their fingers and limbs
agitative, the job the job, ants as the minor keys the swell
of doom, ants run onto the track of brassy and timpani
exoskeletons, in Mahler's grimmest anti-closet ...

She cries out in heart-stopping anty-mezzo Oh believe
O glaube Es geht dir nichts verloren No, you will not
be lost. And only after the heavy chords, only after
burden-bearing back and forth the difference the diff
-erent and the diffident ants (there have to be some
like us): Die as I shall, so as to live! Who isn't moved
by their famous power-to-weight ratio so very serious
(lift and lift! they lift us up! they are the Resurrection!)
Sterben werd' ich um zu leben! sings the soprano,
Yes yes and *ja ja* say the ants.

Philip Salom

Fort Dada

Once off the ship from sector blah blah
she checks into a spa in Baden Baden,
wet air spiced with a pile of old Who's Whos
and warm custardy wafts of ylang ylang.
Only the new filtration system's murmur
and three perfect smiles of pawpaw.
Bowls heaped with wild mushroom couscous
suit the one girl from Wagga Wagga
who knows her rendang from her gado gado.
Bright and rare as a golden bulbul
she caught on quick, so flicked the froufrou,
went off-piste: first tai chi, then the cha cha.
Love's dance, though: now that was lose-lose.
They often wound up tangled in her yoyo.
The holiday in Crete they fought like kri kri,
or way back in the early days in Woy Woy
when she went walkabout with the .22,
blood blurring loud above the never never,
visions surely no one else had had
(her naked papa brandishing his atlatl).
Day-to-day distress remains hush-hush
and being seen wallowing is a booboo—
so Fuck you all, she sighs, and pooh pooh
to the pricks skeptical of my juju ...
Hence the spa, hence the Liszt by Lang Lang.
The diurnal chaconne is in four-four,
night's celloed maestoso, otto-otto.
Autumn shook its crisping ochre pom-pom
when in the thermal mists of Baden Baden
she winked back from her replica tuk tuk
at old sector blah blah, and clinked *cin cin*.

Jaya Savige

Nudge Nudge

Any nuance, any gesture gets me back to this,
Back to the human, back to thinking how it
Comes about I'm here and why, etcetera:
Does it matter? Destined to be dusted into urns, we evoke
Ennui in others. Evening creeps on pads of silent feet on city roofs.
Fat ugly autos prowl the suburb, driven by fat ugly folk.
Get out? Graffiti says 'Why look up here? You are the joke,
Hell isn't others, it's yourself'.
In 2010 all poets were aged thirty, even all of those long dead.
Just joshing. That's my business: I go fishing for bright words,
Kick sounds and ideas round, score goals, get into touch.
Life is after all no graceful sentence but a word.
Most spell it out. A micro-story.
No amount of saying yes negates the fact that no is underrated.
Over time, the mouth that is the origin of trouble
Proves that statues have the best time. No use
Querying their accent. They have earned their right to silence.
Reach no further for the why and how, etcetera,
See life steady see it whole, the gemlike flame that burns us up.
To burn, to live: we tidy up our mums and dads,
Usurp their thrones, their little plots, a little while. The children smile,
Veins full of juice, skin taut: they pole vault over us
While counting: vault or wall-niche, what's the cost?
Xylem feels like that when phloem tips the wink in passing:
You-tube action, up they go, while we go down to sink cells,
Zip from zenith. O the circulatory zing.

Michael Sharkey

Not to be

His quad bike overturns in the creek. Yesterday or tomorrow
the kelpie would have gone for help, but today, today
she is at the vet, today there is no take-back, no near-miss
tall-story germ, only pinned arms and the chassis sinking in
    slimy willow-muck
and thousands of cold brown gallons against his lungs.

 A bloody-minded magpie swoops the kids two paddocks over;
they lie down and kick out at it, legs in the air, backs riding a
    sea of ploughed clods,
just as he'd showed them, laughing and swearing the spring air
    blue. His slowing thoughts of them:
Cheeky buggers. Why can't we go at all our troubles like that, eh? - fuck
    them off
with a swift kick. Not bloody fair. You and your Mum will have the
    insurance, but.

A new silence spreads by the water, ready to fill with questions,
    with words
like *misadventure*, with deep green mud opposing all dredging.
In the end the left-behind can know nothing cleanly, and all
    he knew
is what he wanted for them, and what he didn't want.

Melinda Smith

A Note to Alvaro

You can be happy in Australia as long as you don't go there.
—Alvaro de Campos, June 4, 1931

A poem is a clear defiant thing
and what you wrote in 1931
sounds funny from a naval engineer
who never saw the place where I was born.
You lacked a certain gravitas and calm
unlike your captain friend Pierre Loti.
Yours is a sad bewildered poem.

My home town was pretty much like yours,
a great port on the sea lanes of the world.
I remember the liners, the merchant ships, the yachts,
the wailing of the sirens, the swooping cries of gulls
and fishing boats at morning round the wharves,
the hidden melodies of sea and sky.

Imagined places might be best of all,
perhaps that is what you were saying.
Geography is destiny I've heard.
We do not choose the place where we are born.

Vivian Smith

Nox

A poem addressed to Anne Carson

My husband is wheeled from emergency to theatre
      along a hallway carpeted with silence.
Escorted to a waiting room, almost fin de siècle Victorian,
      I survey medical books encased by glass and
      blighted like old taxidermy.
The registrar, wearing a Freudian beard, stalls at the door,
      unimpressed by my progress in mourning.
The heart has failed, he insists.
He draws a childish diagram on a scrap of paper
      pressed onto the coffee table.
I must strike him as thoughtless, but I am thinking.
Hospitals were not always like this.
When I was a girl, gurney wheels trundled on a bright-and-shine floor
      that disinfected all memory of grief
      —sanitised the griever, whole.
Now, with the registrar spilling words, I am cleaning up after him,
      revising his sentences into tidy units of five or ten,
      repeating the most pleasing combinations again and again.
My fingers type at my side, next to invisible.
The only person who would see them has, by now, been anaesthetised.

I did not invent the typewriter, but at some point in the high school
      typing pool, it secretly invented me:
      aaa space bbb.
Before then, I was silent as a rabbit beneath
      the zig zag of a classroom ceiling,
      enthralled by Pythagorean heaven.
Then suddenly: a surge of electricity.

The machine was oneiric, like good gothic technology.
It brought words to my fingertips—*words, words, words*—
      to be purified through mathematics.
But here the registrar, persisting with his lesson on the heart,
      knows nothing of my scientific art.
When he finally leaves, satisfied I am pathological,
      I remove a laptop from my black bag of tricks,
      usurping the drawing of cardiac arrest.
Nox is not here.
Your book on grief is at home amongst my alphabetised books,
      a perfect accordion sheaf folded in a rectangular box.
You might understand how I compose.
This elegiac poem, recounted just so.

Maria Takolander

Shells

Shells on my shelf are an empty civility
they speak of oceans lost to their memory
but whorled in their spiral architecture
they lure me into something
as complex and better designed
than a legal system, as intricate
as a nation's finances and much
more beautiful. They're dead
replicas of Leptis Magna
grounded on sand. They announce
that their once palpitating citizens
have spawned off, or salted into decay
leaving these bleached wonders, beached
now on my window ledge where a salt-
laden breath of the Indian Ocean
whistles at their open doors.

Andrew Taylor

When I am Gardening, When You Ask

I will tell you that the heart can lie
in dying weeds: a sculpture of twinings,
this crispness says something of the time we have taken

this cooling rips open the wind, these shortenings of day
wait for fire – it is a choice, but I pull out the weeds anyway,
knowing it is you who pulls me inside, then outside again.

Heather Taylor Johnson

Waking

Note the passive voice in that last line,
the denial implied. 'People were shipped out.'
The agent with a conscious brain linked
to a hand with a pen or a gun felt his own grip
all along the neural pathways.

Some noises we can sleep through
but even the softest can be an alarm.
Sailboats in the calmest water are still not swans,
not even, despite voyages and size,
albatrosses. This can only, however,

be a dream resurgent after eighteen years.
Too awake for anything but analysis,
a brain will cling in turmoil to whatever
rock of clarity presents. 'This is not happening'
is not a valid option. Imagine:

not the slow comfort of waking
from nightmare but its opposite.
The colours of no apparent ceremony
covered not only skin but politics,
history. Most of all they hid the will to act.

Tim Thorne

The Habit of Wings

Your grief for what you've lost lifts a mirror
up to where you are bravely working.

Expecting the worst, you look, and instead,
here's the joyful face you've been wanting to see.

Your hand opens and closes and opens and closes.
If it were always a fist or always stretched open,
you would be paralysed.

Your deepest presence is in every small contracting and expanding,
the two as beautifully balanced and coordinated
as birdwings.
—Rumi

Every season is more than itself alone;
Each moment and slow passage of time

Has a twin. Feeling bleak and daunted
All this grey Easter long—doing grief's

Work, as it's best done, alone—I caught
In the mirror, more than once, a man

So much lighter than the man I'd been
Hauling about, like a burlap sack

Of granite, like four decades of dropped
Anchors, and he put me in mind, this other

Self, of a goshawk making ready for flight.
And for a moment, that's stretched

Into a week, I flew, too (thankful for
The mirror and the doubleness of things).

Sometimes one's flown the cage, already,
That holds one in. One heals by bearing

The pain and all the days one's left behind;
One heals by setting them aside. Inside

The stone, there's light; inside the heft
And harrow of all you've lost, a flight

That aches for air. The soul wants,
First, to clench, and then to spread its

Fingers. Love is made of feathers and of
Bone—and healing has the habit of wings.

Mark Tredinnick

Horse

Bending to the earth, the silhouette of a horse
is a hillside, dense as almond wood.
From wither to tail, a bristling escarpment
drops to a levelling range and a broadening flatland,
its bare-blank spine, cradles the sprawling horizon
and valley depths. At first light, with the long
slope of its neck plunging groundward,
it stands steaming among the outcrops,
thawing with the quartz stone earth.
As the sun lifts, the mist comes quietly,
idly avalanching the treetops before draining
into the white void of the morning air.
On ironed hooves and crooked stumps, the horse
stays grazing, dipping and disappearing into itself.
Frostmelt drips from the red-brown furrows of its hide
down into the mud and clover.
                              Blowing in from the tops,
the air shifts and stirs; long flanks of light
strip shadows from the clay. Dozy, not asleep,
the horse sinks further into a wilderness within its skull.
How easily it drifts, stooped under such tonnage,
poised and unmoved in its thickly furred slack frame.
Motionless, under half-closed lids it has slipped,
as if flown from the bars of an unlocked gate,
bolted to the blind spot between its eyes,
dawning headlong deep in the dew.

Todd Turner

Crossing Galata, Istanbul

Flying fish
on Galata Bridge,
rods bowing and bobbing
like suppliants at a vizier's audience.
Each fisher has his own space program,
launch pad,
elbow room, bait bucket,
like this sleeve-tugging city. I'm
for the fish, somehow. Down there
there's piscine stitching of continents: Europe – Asia,
ferries and fish restaurants. Crossing
their sunshine
I pass between poles
of then and now,
a fish caught
in a rip of time, the zip of bait, the
howl of hook in mouth, it flips me
onto this bridge and off, too scrappy a catch,
victim of cheap jet fuel and wanderlust.

John Upton

Even Solomon in All His Glory

Brilliantly bleached sunlets
those big daisies bulge on their bush

the lurid cyclamens are crouched
in squeals of shocking pink

pigface and campanula
contribute their costume jewellery

but raggedy scarlet geraniums
have been out all winter

and don't give a stuff, in their simple way
aping these worn bricks and bluestone:

they are in, you might say
for the long unblushing haul.

Would it were possible
that we could all just keep on

blooming here
like they might long well be.

Ha!
This is mere lament

but I have seized at least
the coarse-barked, fruiting tree of life

and shaken the living daylights
out of its crown.

Chris Wallace-Crabbe

Long-On

A famous big hitter in cricket
Hit his cover drive into the thicket
    Where girls tanned in the nude
    And no gent would intrude,
But Long-on was on a good wicket.
—Douglas Catley

Fielding at Long-on, a ruminant admires
the valley of *eucalyptus ficifolia* in full flower.

1

Long on detail, short
On operational procedure to contain them,
For someone supposedly fielding

In some outfield that will be forever
Offlimits, this vista should beguile the over
With sky motes and beams falling.

2

Long on the minds of that ruminant
Is the untoward forwardness
Of many items in the visual field

Under the lofted sunshower:
The flowering trees towering in the valley,
The persuasively cloudless horizon.

3

Long held notions of grace – such as
The passage of a wake
In ringlets along the furrowing bow –

Propose events at whose horizon
As it were (always *as it were*),
Someone is running in to bowl.

4
Longinus on the Sublime
Might well have noted the vista from here,
A valley of blossoming eucalypt canopies,

Acres of crimson cauliflower,
And leaned into the wind
And missed any number of overthrows.

5
He, that nominal fielder at Long-on,
Student of foliage, registrar of stasis,
Might between overs puzzle over

Elizabeth Bishop's favourite lines of her own:
"All the untidy activity continues
Awful but cheerful."

6
A she-oak at Long-on
Appears to be well within the boundary
Which is, it must be conceded,

Uncertainly marked out with white flags.
It (the she-oak) is a shady lady
Beautiful but indifferent to the game.

7
Long ago this part of the outfield
Was a cold swimming-pool
Fed by mountain springs,

Then was levelled and grassed,
Perhaps at the time this she-oak took root
Where swimmers dived and surfaced.

8

He has become forgetful, this observer,
Musing on the old joke: *a musical umpire*
Sings to a famous melody

"After this ball it's over"
And when over is called, unnoticed,
He stays on longer at Long-on.

9

The longstanding late afternoon light
Draws him increasingly to the valley
And away from the distant batsman

So that he finds himself
Confronted by canopy upon canopy
In a procession of raised torches.

10

Long overdue, a change in bowling;
A pullover is handed to someone
And white trousers run up in the remote

Distant motes and beams.
Long-on is undisturbed and on
The point of strolling towards the she-oak.

11

In the she-oak's curtained shade
Within the uncertain boundaries,
A gingham picnic is underway

As over is called. Mothers and children,
A cloth spread on the ground, suggestions
Of a modest *Lunch on the Grass.*

12
The batsman at the other end
Is preparing to take strike.
A general migration has crisscrossed the pitch.

Even plovers tiptoe in the outfield.
Only Long-on seems rooted to the spot,
A sap-shoot of the she-oak, gazing.

13
Grazing, he is musing over extremes,
Amongst them children's unidiomatic "translations"
Into French, e.g. *sur la façon maison*

For *on the way home.*
He feels similarly displaced and homeless, forgetting
And forgotten out here on the boundary.

14
The cloned eucalypt canopies
Like a curd of eddying weir foam;
Below them fronds and ferns;

And that's only the foreground –
Little wonder that he has his back
To whoever plays a straight bat down the line.

15
And closer by far than where the action is
The valley offers an array of strokes:
Lanceolate, pinnate, palmate, trifoliate –

And that's only where the ball whistles overhead,
Bypassing Long-on,
To be caught by a picnicker.

16
What epiphanies come unbidden
When one is half hidden fielding in shadow?
A squall of rapid pursuit birds

Flies into the arms of the she-oak
Followed by a listening silence...
Then he is distracted, dreaming again.

17
In a vacancy far from the middle
He is considering the children's riddle
In the flare of the flowering trees:

Four blackbirds sitting on a fence,
One is shot. How many are left?
Answer: *None. The others flew away.*

18
And the celebrated Steinberg perspective,
New York in detail and, in the distance, Russia,
Suggests his position here:

He is in his own snowbound, blossoming Russia,
Remote from the batsmen who run a leg bye
In expansive Manhattan sunlight.

19
Longeurs of rose papaya,
Long sunlit shafts through the canopy,
Longings for his own efflorescence

In the face of *eucalyptus ficifolia* folios,
While far away the bails
Tremble but manage not to fall.

John Watson

The Barassi Variations

The Argument: I've met Australian Football's most famous personality a few times and on one occasion he told of a brief sequence of words he had recently heard which, if it were repeated as many times as there were words, with each word emphasised in turn, its meaning would be considerably altered. Thus 'I never said he took the money.'

Theme

To versify my survey on
such alchemy as words contain,
I've thought it through and offer, Ron,
these variants to your refrain
(let's hope witty, maybe punny):
I never said he took the money.

Indignity

I'm the wrong guy. Who me blab?
Have Golden Rules gone all to seed?
Dealer, ponce, pimp, stoolie, scab:
let's vomit 'cause I loathe the breed.
Don't take us for that kind of bunny!
I *never said he took the money.*

True Blue

This man's Aussie and my mate.
You think friendship's passé, quaint?
Allow me to reiterate:

what's my line? Well dobbing ain't!
See here fuckhead, what's so funny?
I never *said he took the money.*

Calligrapher

Find the average talkback grating?
Got a voice and fancy choral?
Though when one's communicating
who's to say it should be aural?
Scrawled on parchment/ in the dunny
I never said *he took the money.*

Heavyweight

Well inside our suspect zone,
But out of order, sync and bounds,
we're looking at a Tyson clone
who could last the fifteen rounds
with Ali, Louis, Dempsey, Tunney.
I never said he *took the money.*

Vocalist

Young man hits the karaoke.
On me! My shout! Freebee! Gratis!
Talent scouts cheer. Almost broke he
nearly turns recording artist,
gets cold feet, walks out on Sony.
I never said he took *the money!*

Schoolmasters

Meanwhile with over-focused eye
pedagogues like swarms of gnats

amplify and specify
theses, thoses, this 'n' thats;
turning grammar, syntax runny:
I never said he took the *money!*

Lothario

The chauvinist rolled out his line:
'All babes love it, I won't hurt you.
Your place equally as mine
to dispose that shrinking virtue?'
Advantage seized? Well maybe honey,
I never said he took the money.

Girl Talk

It's a staple through the ages,
gold-digger teams with sugar pa.
Till in receipt of final wages:
'With men I'm through so ciao 'n' taa.'
Goodtime gal turned out quite nunney.
(Although of course she took the money.)

Alan Wearne

A Quiet Morning

As a man feels an assurance
when getting on a horse and settling
in the curved saddle, knowing
where he is going, the long nose
lighting the way,
Eloise the female executioner
sits squatly with her axe, all arm muscles
ready to ripple. She waits
in the corner of the stage,
eyelids sprung, fingers white.

Ahead of her the field prickles
in the morning light, the stumpy trees,
creamy flowers, circumspect squirrels, the miles and miles of it,
all topped off with a hovering mist.

This afternoon her axe will fall
on the tiny neck of Anne Boleyn.
Eloise does not know if Boleyn deserves her death.
What she knows is that death
already floats upon her like a stream of blue ribbons,
and death's own hands are wrapped round Eloise's.
She is a worker, she works, and when she has struck
death's dying is done.

Petra White

Apollon Musagète

Critic: Tell me, Mr. Balanchine, where did you ever see Apollo on his
*   knees?*
Balanchine: Tell me, Mr. So and So, where did you ever see Apollo?

I. Prologue
All good art begins with a weird birth unseen,
        or seen as dotted rhythms knocking hard on high: here
a mountainous mother, heaving a landslide
        to cushion the fall
out of the swaddling   *massive.*   Quick—coupé
turning point to quaver   weedy limbs.
There will be no dead spots anywhere.

II. Variation of Apollo
The problem of the poem—like the problem of the lute—
can be thawed with play. Instructions:
~ present outwards, unsure of score or strength or harmony;
~ pitch arms wide for a full circle strum;
~ learn the sting of withered efforts and proceed
  body over neck over body with youthful generosity.
These are studied revolutions in attitude and grace.

III. Apollo & the three Muses
A choreographer may tell you this: it always pays
to reinvent oneself, surrounded by women
adept at odd lines—women who *grand battement*
on pointe and stretch their blistered toes to the sun.
Women who insist a flat-footed shuffle, a turned-in leg
or bent pirouette; sharp educators in civil disobedience
offering tutorials in filigree counterpoint:

Variation of Calliope
These hands conduct ecstatic verse from the ribcage
through an over-thought Alexandrine density.
When vision is thin, the chest caves in. (This I know).
If you turn your head, I'll scribble in your sidelines.

Variation of Polyhymnia
sh| gesture can be taught at great speed;
a saucy pirouette with one finger to the lips—
the imagination goes wild. sh| The fun of mime
can be a tonic for new movement; the danger is
                        (mouth flung wide)   O ||

Variation of Terpsichore
One must use the stage wisely to reveal
the body's jigsaw precision: here are the hips,
twisty as a soda top; the arms breezy; tendons flexed.
The dance is lean-revelation and pluck; the body is a neat thing.

Apollo is opening, closing his fist—neon
     flashing lights—and now he knows *this*
about kick and control; subtle liaisons
     of language and line. Let us go, he says,
for a slow walk, or a swimming lesson, or frisky
     diversions in the troika. Bounce the strings
fast and strong enough to test our laurels without
     fear of fall or rest within the score.
His attention is drawn wide as a curtain
     on a New York apartment window.

IV. Apotheosis

Adolescence is a half-hour exertion—so it seems
what's hard is best learned fast. To dare not use
everything but draw together certain family relations ·
in one's art: music, movement, humour—
humble pie and vodka   with a side of disagreement

cut short.   (We'll continue the conversation upstairs).

Jessica L. Wilkinson

Based upon the choreography of George Balanchine, 1928 and music of Igor
Stravinsky, 1927/28

The First Four Hours

Give me six hours to chop down a tree, and I will spend the
first four sharpening the axe.
   —unknown; often misattributed to Abraham Lincoln

However blunt the blade was
to begin with, one must admit:
the time allocated to undertake the task

seems excessive. Four hours
with the stovepipe hat set aside, the shirtsleeves
rolled, four hours whistling as he held

the weapon to the whetstone's happy edge
or brought it to the wheel, then depressed
and depressed his hefty boot,

scraping out sparks in a celebratory
cascade. He must have stopped
every so often to roll his shoulders, to stretch

the presidential neck and quadriceps —
nevertheless, patience is the lesson,
patience while his waistcoat darkens

from perspiration, while he ignores
a sacral ache, patience while state business
remains in stasis, patience while the thing

is whittled sharper than the republican
cheekbones from which his gravitas hung. Surely
there comes a point at which the thing

can be no keener, when the dream
of raw timber becomes sweeter
than any genuine sap could be, varnishing

one's palms with its dark, deciduous gleam.
There must be a moment in which
preparation extends past itself,

past readiness, into the pleasure inherent
in tension; some unstatesmanlike frisson,
too impolitic to mention.

Chloe Wilson

A queer and sultry summer

For Maddie

There's a fig tree tattooed on your hipbone,
but you want, almost,
the fruit to fall,
for the way the seeds within your belly burn,

that stalklike feeling in the throat.
The waiter asks if we ate too much chocolate over Easter.
You don't order, I still put saccharine
in my coffee. Your roommates
hid your gym shoes for the long weekend,
     and we complain
about our families who forget we're not unharmed
or let us know how strongly
they are willing us to health:
it's an investment, mine say.
In dud stocks, I often think, although it's how they show
they give a fig. I can't resolve

your need, but feel it spit against my windscreen
the whole way home.
You wear a talisman that scares you.
  A dress to match your orange shoes.

I read, that afternoon, that a fig
is just a mulberry turned inside-out;
perhaps we're silkless.
  But there are things
I want for you:

fig jam, fig paste, poached figs, stewed figs, stuffed figs,
a sticky harvest.

      The ability
to eat them from the ground.

Fiona Wright

III

death was such good fun –
        booze, drugs & poetry.

how did i avoid you?
        so Byronic, so good looking!

i've grown old & lucky
        but still there's too many of me,

scratching marks on paper, computers,
        Beethoven, the horses of Lascaux.

there's wars for the young but
        still our population grows.

spring, & purple flowers spatter the horizon –
        i like it here & don't want to leave

Rae Desmond Jones

Publication Details

Fay Zwicky's 'In Memoriam, JB' appeared in *Kenyon Review*, Volume 39, Number 2, March 2017.

Robert Adamson's 'Winter, Hospital Bed' appeared in *POETRY*, November 2017.

Jordie Albiston's 'cobalt' appeared in *Verity La*, 14 October 2016.

Cassandra Atherton's 'Gypsy' appeared in *Antic*, January 2017.

Luke Beesley's 'Reunion Song' appeared in *Cordite Poetry Review*, 1 February 2017.

Judith Beveridge's 'Flying Foxes, Wingham Brush' appeared in *Island*, Issue 150, September 2017.

Judith Bishop's 'The Grey Parrot' appeared in *Australian Book Review*, Number 386, November 2016.

Kim Cheng Boey's 'Time is a river, time is a bridge' appeared in *Cordite Poetry Review*, 1 November 2016.

Ken Bolton's 'Reach & Ambition' appeared in *Cordite Poetry Review*, 1 May 2017.

Peter Boyle's 'Eleutheria' appeared in his collection *Ghostspeaking*, Vagabond Press, Sydney, August 2016.

Margaret Bradstock's 'Forty-one degrees' appeared in *Quadrant*, Volume 61, Number 4, April 2017.

Lisa Brockwell's 'The Shower Stall' appeared in *Loving Kindness: Poems from the ACU 2016 Prize for Poetry*, Bambra Press, Port Melbourne, September 2016.

David Brooks's 'The Night Coming' appeared *Kenyon Review*, Volume 39, Number 2, March 2017.

Pam Brown's 'Soft Targets' appeared in *Past Simple*, Issue 12, May 2017.

Joanne Burns's 'compensation' appeared in the *Journal of Poetics Research*, 16 September 2016.

Michelle Cahill's 'Minor Domestic' appeared in her collection *The Herring Loss*, Arc Publications, Todmorden, October 2016.

Lee Cataldi's 'c'est l'homme' appeared in *Cordite Poetry Review*, 1 May 2017.

Julie Chevalier's 'another step away' appeared in *Meanjin*, Volume 76, Issue 1, Autumn 2017.

Eileen Chong's 'Kumera' appeared in *Peril*, 25 May 2017.

Jennifer Compton's 'Two Women' appeared in *Australian Poetry Anthology*, Volume 5, Australian Poetry, Melbourne, April 2017.

Stuart Cooke's 'Fallen Myrtle Trunk' appeared in *Rochford Street Review*, 1 December 2016.

Shevaun Cooley's 'meadows empty of him, animal eyes, impersonal as glass' appeared in his collection *Homing*, Giramondo, Sydney, May 2017.

Judith Crispin's 'Five Threnodies for Maralinga: Part III' appeared in *Axon: Creative Explorations*, Capsule 1 (Special Issue), August 2016.

Sarah Day's 'Reservoir' appeared in *Cordite Poetry Review*, 1 May 2017.

Shastra Deo's 'I Saw the Devil in the Cane Fields' appeared in *Meanjin*, Volume 76, Issue 2, Winter 2017.

B.R. Dionysius's 'Barnacle' appeared in *Tremble: The University of Canberra Vice-Chancellor's International Poetry Prize 2016*, International Poetry Studies Institute, Canberra, September 2016.

Lucy Dougan's 'The Throne' appeared in *Strange Cargo: Five Australian Poets*, Smith|Doorstop books, Huddersfield, June 2017.

Laurie Duggan's 'Six Afterimages' appeared in the *Journal of Poetics Research*, 1 August 2016.

Adrienne Eberhard's 'Distance' appeared in *Australian Book Review's Tasmanian States of Poetry 2016 Anthology*, April 2017.

Ali Cobby Eckermann's 'The Apology Day breakfast' appeared in *Overland*, Issue 227, Winter 2017.

Stephen Edgar's 'La Vita Nuova' appeared in *Kenyon Review*, Volume 39, Number 2, March 2017.

Anne Elvey's 'Putting on your boots' appeared in *Southerly*, Volume 76, Issue 2, January 2017.

Russell Erwin's 'Because, like the weather' appeared in *Quadrant*, Volume 61, Number 6, June 2017.

Diane Fahey's 'The Art of Birds' appeared in *Axon: Creative Explorations*, Capsule 1 (Special Issue), August 2016.

Michael Farrell's 'The Snake' appeared in *Plumwood Mountain*, Volume 4, Number 2, August 2017.

Susan Fealy's 'For Cornflowers to Sing' appeared in the *Weekend Australian*, 18 February 2017.

Liam Ferney's 'Main Street Social' appeared in *Australian Book Review's Queensland States of Poetry 2017 Anthology*, October 2017.

Luke Fischer's 'Stones' appeared in his collection *A Personal History of Vision*, UWA Publishing, Perth, February 2017.

Toby Fitch's '27 Materialisations of Sydney Cloud' appeared in *Island*, Issue 151, November 2017.

John Foulcher's 'Before the Storm' appeared in *Australian Book Review's ACT States of Poetry 2017 Anthology*, April 2017.

William Fox's 'The Western District' appeared in *Meanjin*, Volume 76, Issue 1, Autumn 2017.

Angela Gardner's 'Unkempt if You Will' appeared in *Cordite Poetry Review*, 1 August 2017.

Lisa Gorton's 'Empirical VII' appeared in *Australian Book Review's Victoria States of Poetry 2017 Anthology*, April 2017.

Phillip Hall's 'Inheritance' appeared in *Southerly*, Volume 76, Issue 2, January 2017.

Natalie Harkin's 'Heart's Core Lament' appeared in *Australian Poetry Journal*, Issue 7, Number 1, June 2017.

Jennifer Harrison's 'The Tent' appeared in the *Weekend Australian*, 14 January 2017.

Dimitra Harvey's 'Acrocorinth' appeared in *Philament Journal*, Issue 22, December 2016.

John Hawke's 'Zero Degrees' appeared in *Australian Book Review*, Number 386, November 2016.

Dominique Hecq's 'The Hanged Man' appeared in *Meniscus*, Volume 5, Issue 1, June 2017.

Paul Hetherington's 'Inchings and Belongings: After Paul Strand' appeared in *Westerly*, Volume 61, Number 2, November 2016.

Barry Hill's 'Mister Lincoln or Camp David' appeared in the *Weekend Australian*, 22 July 2017.

Andy Jackson's 'Song not for you' appeared in *Cordite Poetry Review*, 1 November 2016.

Clive James's 'Head Wound' appeared in *Kenyon Review*, Volume 39, Number 2, March 2017.

Carol Jenkins's 'Barns in Charlevoix' appeared in *Cordite Poetry Review*, 1 May 2017.

A. Frances Johnson's 'Greenfield development' appeared in the *Canberra Times*, 4 March 2017.

Jill Jones's 'Murray andante' appeared in *Griffith Review*, Edition 55, January 2017.

Amanda Joy's 'Almost Pause/ Pareidolia' appeared in her collection *Snake Like Charms*, UWA Publishing, Perth, February 2017.

Carmen Leigh Keates's 'To Paint the Inside of a Church' appeared in *Axon: Creative Explorations*, Volume 6, Number 2, November 2016.

Antigone Kefala's 'On Loss' appeared in her collection *Fragments*, Giramondo, Sydney, August 2016.

John Kinsella's 'A New Norcia Subset' appeared in *Westerly*, Volume 62, Number 1, July 2017.

Louis Klee's 'Windborne Avenue' appeared in *Meanjin*, Volume 75, Issue 3, Spring 2016.

Mike Ladd's 'The Corpse Flower Sketch' appeared in the *Weekend Australian*, 21 January 2017.

Anthony Lawrence's 'A Tasting' appeared in his collection *101 Poems*, Pitt Street Poetry, Sydney, November 2017.

Bronwyn Lea's 'Zeitgeist' appeared in *Australian Book Review*, Number 391, May 2017.

Jeanine Leane's 'Over the River Memory' appeared in *Rabbit Poetry Journal*, Issue 21, May 2017.

Emma Lew's 'Rattling the Forms' appeared in *Cordite Poetry Review*, 1 August 2017.

Cassie Lewis's 'In Memoriam' appeared in her collection *The Blue Decodes*, Grand Parade Poets, Sydney, October 2016.

Bella Li's 'The Novelist Elena Ferrante' appeared in her collection *Argosy*, Vagabond Press, Sydney, February 2017.

Jennifer Maiden's 'Metronome' appeared in her collection *The Metronome*, Giramondo, Sydney, March 2017.

Caitlin Maling's 'Fisheries Raid' appeared in *Rabbit Poetry Review*, Issue 19, November 2016.

David McCooey's 'One Way or Another' appeared in his collection *Star Struck*, UWA Publishing, Perth, October 2016.

Peter Minter's 'Remembering Sandstone Country' appeared in *Kenyon Review*, Volume 39, Number 2, March 2017.

Marjon Mossammaparast's 'The Spanish Revelation' appeared in *Cordite Poetry Review*, 18 June 2017.

Philip Neilsen's 'Anna Karenina' appeared in *Island*, Issue 149, May 2017.

Geoff Page's 'Bombala' appeared in *Quadrant*, Volume 60, Issue 9, September 2016.

Claire Potter's 'The Hidden Side to Love' appeared in *Meanjin*, Volume 75, Issue 4, Summer 2016.

Ron Pretty's 'Pigeons of the Dome' appeared in *Quadrant*, Volume 61, Number 3, March 2017.

Brendan Ryan's 'The Lowlands of Moyne' appeared in *Antipodes*, Volume 31, Number 1, July 2017.

Gig Ryan's 'Muzzled Altar' appeared in *Kenyon Review*, Volume 39, Number 2, March 2017.

Tracy Ryan's 'Homeschooling' appeared in the *Weekend Australian*, 3 December 2016.

Philip Salom's 'Strange Music' appeared in *Kenyon Review*, Volume 39, Number 2, March 2017.

Jaya Savige's 'Fort Dada' appeared in *Kenyon Review* Volume 39, Number 2, March 2017.

Michael Sharkey's 'Nudge Nudge' appeared in *Snorkel*, Issue 23, September 2016.

Melinda Smith's 'Not to be' appeared in *Island*, Issue 146, September 2016.

Vivian Smith's 'A Note to Alvaro' appeared in *Quadrant*, Volume 61, Issue 7/8, July 2017.

Maria Takolander's 'Nox' appeared in *Cordite Poetry Review*, 1 August 2016.

Andrew Taylor's 'Shells' appeared in his collection *Impossible Preludes*, Margaret River Press, Witchcliffe, October 2016.

Heather Taylor Johnson's 'When I am Gardening, When You Ask' appeared in the *Weekend Australian*, 3 September 2016.

Tim Thorne's 'Waking' appeared in *Australian Book Review's Tasmanian States of Poetry 2016 Anthology*, April 2017.

Mark Tredinnick's 'The Habit of Wings' appeared in *Axon: Creative Explorations*, Capsule 1 (Special Issue), August 2016.

Todd Turner's 'Horse' appeared in the *Weekend Australian*, 7 January 2017.

John Upton's 'Crossing Galata, Istanbul' appeared in *Overland*, Issue 227, Winter 2017.

Chris Wallace-Crabbe's 'Even Solomon in All His Glory' appeared in *Kenyon Review*, Volume 39, Number 2, March 2017.

John Watson's 'Long-On' appeared in *The Danger Island garbage boat*, Hunter Writers Centre, Newcastle, October 2016.

Alan Wearne's 'The Barassi Variations' appeared in his collection *These Things Are Real*, Giramondo, Sydney, July 2017.

Petra White's 'A Quiet Morning' appeared in her collection *Reading for a Quiet Morning*, Gloria SMH Press, Melbourne, May 2017.

Jessica L. Wilkinson's 'Apollon Musagète' appeared in *Cordite Poetry Review*, 1 March 2017.

Chloe Wilson's 'The First Four Hours' appeared in *Cordite Poetry Review*, 1 May 2017.

Fiona Wright's 'A queer and sultry summer' appeared in *Shaping the Fractured Self: poetry of chronic illness and pain*, UWA Publishing, Perth, May 2017.

Rae Desmond Jones's 'III' appeared in his collection *A Caterpillar on a Leaf*, Puncher and Wattmann, Sydney, 2016.

Notes on Contributors

THE EDITOR

Sarah Holland-Batt is an award-winning poet, critic, editor and academic. Her most recent book of poems, *The Hazards* (UQP), won the 2016 Prime Minister's Literary Award for Poetry, and was shortlisted for the New South Wales Premier's Kenneth Slessor Prize, the AFAL John Bray Memorial Poetry Award, the Queensland Literary Awards Judith Wright Calanthe Award, and the Western Australian Premier's Book Awards. She is the recipient of the W.G. Walker Memorial Fulbright Scholarship, fellowships from Yaddo and MacDowell colonies in the United States, the Australia Council Literature Residency at the B.R. Whiting Studio in Rome, and a Sidney Myer Creative Fellowship, among other honours. She presently lives in Brisbane, where she works as a senior lecturer in creative writing at QUT, and the poetry editor of *Island*.

POETS

Fay Zwicky (1933–2017) published nine books of poetry, the most recent of which is her *Collected Poems*, edited by Lucy Dougan and Tim Dolin (UWAP, 2017). She also edited several anthologies of Australian poetry, published a book of short stories, *Hostages* (FACP, 1983), and a collection of critical essays, *The Lyre in the Pawnshop* (UWAP, 1986). Her many awards include the NSW Premier's Award, the WA Premier's Award, the Patrick White Award and the Christopher Brennan Award.

Robert Adamson's latest collection of poetry, *Net Needle*, was published by Black Inc. in Australia and by Flood Editions in the USA in May 2015, and by Bloodaxe Books in the UK in May 2016. It was shortlisted for the Queensland Premier's Poetry Award and the Prime Minister's Literary Awards. At the Sydney Writers' Festival in May 2016, Adamson launched an Australian issue of *Poetry*, which he edited with Don Share, editor of Chicago's Poetry Foundation. He edited Black Inc.'s *The Best Australian Poems 2009* and *The Best Australian Poems 2010*.

Jordie Albiston has published ten poetry collections and a handbook on poetic form. Albiston possesses an ongoing pre-occupation with mathematical constructs and constraints, and the possibilities offered in terms of poetic structure. Her work has won many awards, including the Mary Gilmore Award and the 2010 NSW Premier's Prize. She lives in Melbourne.

Cassandra Atherton is a prose-poet and scholar. She was a Harvard Visiting Scholar in English in 2016 and has been awarded a VicArts and Australian Council Grant for her prose poetry on the atomic bomb. She has written eight books and is the poetry editor of *Westerly*.

Luke Beesley is a Melbourne-based poet. His most recent collection is *Jam Sticky Vision* (Giramondo, 2015). His fifth collection, *Aqua Spinach* (Giramondo), is forthcoming.

Judith Beveridge is the author of six award-winning collections. Her *New and Selected Poems* will appear in 2018. She was a recipient of the Philip Hodgins Memorial Medal in 2005 and was the poetry editor for *Meanjin* during 2005–2015. Her work has been widely anthologised and translated.

Judith Bishop is a poet and professional linguist. Her first poetry collection, *Event*, won the Anne Elder award and was shortlisted for the CJ Dennis Prize, the Judith Wright Calanthe Award, and the ASAL Mary Gilmore Prize. A second collection, *Interval*, is forthcoming from UQP in March 2018.

Kim Cheng Boey was born in Singapore and migrated to Australia in 1997. He taught Creative Writing at the University of Newcastle for 13 years, before returning to Singapore as an Associate Professor in English at Nanyang Technological University. He has published five collections of poetry, a travel memoir entitled *Between Stations*, as well as a historical novel on the life of the Tang Dynasty poet Du Fu.

Ken Bolton – what's to say? His most recent books are *Lonnie's Lament* from Wakefield Press, *London Journal/London Poem* from Vagabond and *Threefer* from Puncher & Wattmann. He lives in Adelaide.

Peter Boyle is a Sydney-based poet and translator of poetry. He is the author of seven books of poetry, most recently *Ghostspeaking*, which won the 2017 Kenneth Slessor poetry Prize. He has translated poetry by José Kozer, Marosa di Giorgio and Eugenio Montejo, among others.

Margaret Bradstock has six published collections of poetry, including *The Pomelo Tree* (winner of the Wesley Michel Wright Prize) and *Barnacle Rock* (winner of the Woollahra Festival Award, 2014). Editor of *Antipodes* (2011) and *Caring for Country* (2017), Margaret won the Banjo Paterson Poetry Award in 2014, 2015 and 2017.

Lisa Brockwell lives on a rural property near Byron Bay with her husband and young son. She was runner-up in the University of Canberra Vice-Chancellor's International Poetry Prize in 2015. Her first collection, *Earth Girls*, published by Pitt Street Poetry in 2016, was commended in the Anne Elder Award.

David Brooks's most recent collections are *Open House* (poetry, UQP, 2015), *Napoleon's Roads* (short fiction, UQP, 2016) and *Derrida's Breakfast* (essays, Brandl & Schlesinger, 2016).

Pam Brown is an editor, reviewer and author of various chapbooks and pamphlets as well as many books of poetry. A new collection, *Click here for what we do*, is due from Vagabond Press in 2018. She lives in Alexandria, Sydney.

Joanne Burns is a Sydney poet. Her most recent poetry collection *Brush* (Giramondo Publishing, 2014) won the 2016 NSW Premier's Literary Awards Kenneth Slessor Poetry Prize. She is working towards a new collection, *Apparently*, as well as assembling a selected volume of her work, *Real Land*.

Michelle Cahill is a Sydney poet and critic. Her debut fiction *Letter to Pessoa* won the NSW Premier's Literary Award for New Writing and was shortlisted for the Steele Rudd Award. Her work appears in the *Forward Book of Poetry* 2018.

Lee Cataldi has been a teacher and a linguist and has edited a collection of Warlpiri narratives and compiled a dictionary of the Ngardi language. Her three books of poetry have won the Ann Elder award, the Human Rights prize and the NSW Premier's Prize respectively.

Julie Chevalier writes poetry and short fiction in Sydney. Her second poetry collection, *Darger: his girls* (Puncher &Wattmann, 2012), was awarded the Alec Bolton Prize for an Unpublished Poetry Manuscript, and shortlisted for the WA Premier's Poetry Prize. *Permission to Lie*, a short story collection, was published by Spineless Wonders.

Eileen Chong is a Sydney poet. Her books have been shortlisted for several prizes, including the Anne Elder Award, the Prime Minister's Literary Award and the Victorian Premier's Literary Award. Her latest collection, *Another Language*, is with George Braziller in New York.

Jennifer Compton lives in Melbourne and is a poet and playwright who also writes prose. Five Islands Press published her book of poetry, *Now You Shall Know*, in 2014. The title poem won the Newcastle Poetry Prize in 2013.

Stuart Cooke's latest poetry collection is *Opera* (Five Islands Press, 2016). He lives on the Gold Coast, where he lectures at Griffith University. 'Fallen Myrtle Trunk' was the winner of the 2016 New Shoots Poetry Prize.

Shevaun Cooley is a Western Australian poet, essayist, and climber. Her poetry has been published in *Cordite, Island, Poetry Wales, Meanjin, Southerly*, and more, and her work shortlisted for both the Newcastle Poetry Prize, and University of Canberra Vice-Chancellor's International Poetry Prize. Her debut collection, *Homing*, was released in 2017.

Judith Crispin is a poet and photographer. Her works are variously published and exhibited in Australia and Europe. Judith's first collection of poetry, *The Myrrh-Bearers*, was published in 2015 by Puncher and Wattmann. Her newest book, *The Lumen Seed, photographs, poems and commentaries*, was published by Daylight Books (January 2017).

Sarah Day's most recent book is *Tempo* (Puncher & Wattmann, 2014). It won the Michel Wesley Wright Award and was shortlisted for the Prime Minister's Awards.

Shastra Deo was born in Fiji, raised in Melbourne, and lives in Brisbane, Australia. Her work has appeared in *Cordite, Mascara, Meanjin, Peril*, and elsewhere. Her first book, *The Agonist* (UQP, 2017), won the 2016 Arts Queensland Thomas Shapcott Poetry Prize.

B. R. Dionysius was born in 1969 in Dalby. He has since lived in Ipswich and Brisbane where he is an English teacher at Ipswich Grammar School, was founding Director of the Queensland Poetry Festival and in his spare time watches birds.

Lucy Dougan's books include *White Clay* (Giramondo, 2008), *Meanderthals* (Web del Sol, 2011) and *The Guardians* (Giramondo, 2015). In 2016 *The Guardians* won the Western Australian Premier's Book Award.

Laurie Duggan was born in Melbourne and was involved in the poetry worlds of that city and Sydney. In 2006 he moved to England and currently lives in Faversham, Kent. He has published some twenty books of poems, the most recent being *No Particular Place To Go* (Shearsman, 2017), *Allotments* (Shearsman, 2014), and a reissue of his first two books as *East & Under the Weather* (Puncher & Wattman, 2014).

Adrienne Eberhard's third collection, *This Woman*, was shortlisted for the 2013 Tasmania Book Prize. A new collection is forthcoming from Black Pepper. She is currently writing poems spoken by Marie Antoinette and her contemporary, Marie Girardin, who sailed in Tasmanian waters disguised as a man in 1792/93.

Ali Cobby Eckermann is a Yankunytjatjara Aboriginal poet. She is the author of seven books, including the verse novel *Ruby Moonlight* (Magabala Books, 2012; Flood Editions, 2015), the poetry collection *Inside My Mother* (Giramondo Publishing, 2015), and the memoir *Too Afraid to Cry* (Ilura Press, 2013). In 2017 she was awarded Yale University's Windham Campbell Prize in Poetry.

Stephen Edgar's most recent book is *Transparencies* (Black Pepper, 2017). His previous two books, *Exhibits of the Sun* and *Eldershaw*, were both shortlisted for the Prime Minister's Literary Awards.

Anne Elvey is author of *Kin* (FIP, 2014) and managing editor of *Plumwood Mountain: An Australian Journal of Ecopoetry and Ecopoetics*. *White on White* is forthcoming from *Cordite Books* in early 2018. She holds honorary appointments at Monash University and University of Divinity.

Russell Erwin is a farmer in the Southern Tablelands of NSW. He has had five books published, the most recent being *Maps of Small Countries* (Gininderra Press, 2016).

Diane Fahey is the author of twelve poetry collections, most recently *A House by the River*. She has been awarded various poetry prizes and international residencies, and received literary grants from the Australia Council, and the Victorian and South Australian Governments. She lives in Clifton Springs in Victoria.

Michael Farrell's books include *A Lyrebird: Selected Poems, Cocky's Joy, I Love Poetry*, and *Writing Australian Unsettlement: Modes of Poetic Invention 1796–1945*. He co-edited *Out of the Box: Contemporary Australian Gay and Lesbian Poets*. Originally from Bombala, NSW, Michael lives in Melbourne. He edits *Flash Cove*.

Susan Fealy is a Melbourne-based poet, reviewer, clinical psychologist and fellow in psychiatry at the University of Melbourne. This year she featured at the Perth Poetry Festival and Poetry on the Move (University of Canberra). Her first collection, *Flute of Milk* (UWAP, 2017), won the 2017 Wesley Michel Wright Prize.

Liam Ferney's most recent collection *Content* (Hunter Publishing, 2016) was shortlisted for the Judith Wright Calanthe Award. His previous collection, *Boom* (Grand Parade Poets, 2013), was shortlisted for the Kenneth Slessor Poetry Prize and the Judith Wright Calanthe Award. He is a media manager, poet and aspiring left back living in Brisbane, Australia.

Luke Fischer's books include *A Personal History of Vision* (UWAP Poetry, 2017), *Paths of Flight* (Black Pepper, 2013), and the monograph *The Poet as Phenomenologist: Rilke and the New Poems* (Bloomsbury, 2015). He is an honorary associate in philosophy at the University of Sydney.

Toby Fitch is poetry editor for *Overland*. He lives in Sydney where he works as a teacher and an organiser of poetry events. His books include *Rawshock*, which won the Grace Leven Prize for Poetry 2012, *Jerilderies*, and *The Bloomin' Notions of Other & Beau* (Vagabond, 2016).

John Foulcher has published eleven books of poetry, the most recent being *A Casual Penance* (Pitt Street Poetry, 2017) and *101 Poems* (Pitt Street Poetry, 2016), the latter a selection from his other books. For over thirty-five years, his poems have appeared in magazines, newspapers and anthologies throughout Australia. He lives in Canberra.

William Fox is a poet from Melbourne. His work has been published in *Meanjin, Overland, Southerly, Island*, the *Age*, previous *The Best Australian Poems* editions, and elsewhere.

Angela Gardner is the author of four poetry collections. Her first poetry collection *Parts of Speech* (UQP, 2007) won the Arts Queensland Thomas Shapcott Poetry Prize, then followed *Views of The Hudson* (Shearsman Books UK, 2009). Her most recent collections are *The Told World* (Shearsman Books UK, 2014) and *Thing&Unthing* (Vagabond Press, 2014). She is a visual artist with work in major public collections. She edits the poetry journal *foam:e*.

Lisa Gorton lives in Melbourne and writes poetry, fiction and essays. Her most recent publications, both from Giramondo, are the poetry collection *Hotel Hyperion* and a novel, *The Life of Houses*.

Phillip Hall lives in Melbourne's Sunshine where he is a passionate member of the Western Bulldogs Football Club. His publications include *Diwurruwurru: Poetry from the Gulf of Carpentaria* (Blank Rune Press) and *Borroloola Class* (IPSI). *Fume*, a collection of essays and poetry celebrating Carpentaria's First Australians, is forthcoming with UWAP.

Natalie Harkin is a Narungga woman from South Australia. She is an academic and activist-poet with an interest in the state's colonial archives. Her words have been installed in several exhibitions and she has written for *Overland, Southerly* and *Cordite*. Her manuscript *Dirty Words* was published by Cordite Books in 2015.

Dr. Jennifer Harrison has published seven poetry collections, most recently the chapbook *Air Variations* (University of Canberra, 2017). Her eighth collection *Anywhy* is forthcoming from Black Pepper Press, Melbourne. In 2012 she was awarded the Christopher Brennan Award for sustained achievement in Australian poetry.

Dimitra Harvey has a MA in creative writing from the University of Sydney. Her poetry has appeared in *Meanjin, Southerly, Mascara*, and *Cordite* as well as anthologies such as *The Stars Like Sand* and *A Patch of Sun*. In 2012, she won the ASA's Ray Koppe Young Writer's Residency.

John Hawke teaches literary studies at Monash University. His volume of poetry, *Aurelia* (Cordite Books), won the Anne Elder Award.

Dominique Hecq has a PhD in literary studies, and a background in languages, psychoanalysis and translation. She is the author of thirteen full-length creative works. *Hush: A Fugue* is her latest book of poetry (UWAP, 2017).

Paul Hetherington has published eleven full-length poetry collections and six chapbooks. He won the 2014 Western Australian Premier's Book Awards (poetry) and was shortlisted for the 2017 Kenneth Slessor Prize for Poetry. He is head of the International Poetry Studies Institute at the University of Canberra.

Barry Hill has won Premier's Awards for poetry, non-fiction and the essay. His most recent poetry books are *Grass Hut Work* and *Naked Clay: Drawing from Lucian Freud*, which was shortlisted for the 2013 UK Forward Prize. He was poetry editor for the *Australian* from 1999–2009.

Andy Jackson has featured at literary events and arts festivals in Australia, India, USA and Ireland, and lives in Castlemaine. His most recent collection, *Music our bodies can't hold* (Hunter Publishers, 2017), consists of portrait poems of other people with Marfan Syndrome.

Clive James is the author or more than thirty books. As well as his three volumes of autobiography, he has published collections of literary and television criticism, essays, travel writing, verse and novels. His latest poetry collection is *Nerfertiti in the Flak Tower* (Pan Macmillan, 2012).

Carol Jenkins lives in Sydney. She has published two collections of poetry *Fishing in the Devonian* and *X to the N* and an illustrated episodic novel *Select Episodes from the Mr Farmhand Series*, all from Puncher and Wattmann.

A. Frances Johnson is an award-winning poet, novelist and painter. In 2015 she won the Jospephine Ulrick Poetry Prize. She is a 2017 recipient of the Australia Council writing residency to Rome. Her third book of poetry, *Rendition for Harp and Kalashnikov* is forthcoming with Puncher and Wattmann (2017).

Jill Jones's most recent books include *Breaking the Days*, shortlisted for the 2017 Kenneth Slessor Award, *The Beautiful Anxiety*, winner of the Victorian Premiers' Literary Award for Poetry in 2015, and a chapbook, *The Leaves Are My Sisters*. She is a member of the J.M. Coetzee Centre for Creative Practice, University of Adelaide.

Amanda Joy was born and raised in the Kimberley and Pilbara regions of Western Australia. Her first full-length book, *Snake Like Charms*, including 'Almost Pause/ Pareidolia,' was part of the UWAP Poetry series. Her poem 'Tailings' won the 2016 Peter Porter Poetry Prize. She is the author of two chapbooks, *Not Enough to Fold* and *Orchid Poems*.

Carmen Leigh Keates was the winner of the 2015 Whitmore Press Manuscript Prize, leading to the publication of her critically praised first collection, *Meteorites*. Carmen was awarded her PhD in writing from UQ and has received support from Arts QLD and the Australia Council for the Arts.

Antigone Kefala is a poet and prose writer. Born in Romania of Greek parents, Antigone arrived in Sydney via Greece and New Zealand. She has published several collections of poetry and prose including *Absence* (Hale & Iremonger, 1992), *Fragments* (Giramondo Publishing, 2016) and *Sydney Journals* (Giramondo Publishing, 2008).

John Kinsella has published many volumes of poetry, most recently *On the Outskirts* (UQP, 2017). He is professor of literature and environment at Curtin University, and a fellow of Churchill College, Cambridge University.

Louis Klee is a writer who lives on Wurundjeri country. He won the Peter Porter Prize in 2017.

Mike Ladd lives and writes in Adelaide. He ran *Poetica* on ABC Radio National for two decades and currently makes radio documentaries for RN. His most recent collection of poetry and prose is *Invisible Mending*, published by Wakefield Press in 2016.

Anthony Lawrence's *101 Poems* is forthcoming from Pitt Street Poetry in 2017. His poetry has won many awards, including the Philip Hodgins Memorial Medal, the NSW Premier's Award, the Newcastle Poetry Prize and the Blake Poetry Prize. He is currently completing a book of prose poems.

Bronwyn Lea's books include *Flight Animals* (UQP), *The Other Way Out* (Giramondo), and *The Deep North* (George Braziller). She is poetry editor at *Meanjin* and teaches contemporary literature at the University of Queensland.

Jeanine Leane is a Wiradjuri poet, author and academic from the Murrumbidgee River on the road to Gundagai. Her poetry has appeared in *Southerly*, *Australian Book Review*, *Hecate*, *Contemporary Australian Poetry*, *Australian Poetry Journal* and *Overland*. Jeanine teaches creative writing and aboriginal literature at the University of Melbourne.

Emma Lew lives in Melbourne. Her *New and Selected Poems* will be published in 2018 by Giramondo.

Cassie Lewis is a Melbourne poet currently living in Rochester, New York. She is the author of *The Blue Decodes* (Grand Parade Poets, 2016).

Bella Li is the author of *Maps, Cargo* (Vagabond Press, 2013) and *Argosy* (Vagabond Press, 2017) – a book of poetry, photography and collage. She is a managing co-editor at *Five Islands Press*, as well as a recent guest editor of *Cordite Poetry Review* (Issue 55: Future Machines).

Jennifer Maiden has published twenty-two poetry collections and five novels, and has won three Kenneth Slessors; two C.J. Dennis'; Victorian Prize for Literature; two the *Age* Poetry Books of Years; the *Age* Book of Year; the Christopher Brennan; ALS Gold Medal; and has been shortlisted for The Griffin Poetry Prize. Her latest collection is *Appalachian Fall* (Quemar Press).

Caitlin Maling is a Western Australian poet with two books out through Fremantle Press. She is the current holder of the Marten Bequest in poetry.

David McCooey is a prize-winning poet, critic, and editor. His latest book of poems, *Star Struck*, was published by UWA Publishing in 2016. He is also a musician and composer. His latest album, *The Double*, was released as a digital download in 2017.

Peter Minter is a poet, poetry editor and writer about poetry and poetics. He teaches at the University of Sydney.

Marjon Mossammaparast is a poet and teacher living in Melbourne. Her poetry has appeared in a range of publications over the last decade. She is currently working on her first collection through Cordite Books.

Philip Neilsen will have his sixth collection of poetry, *Wildlife of Berlin*, published in 2018 by UWAP. He is adjunct professor of creative writing at QUT and teaches poetics at the University of Queensland.

Geoff Page is based in Canberra. He has published twenty-three collections of poetry as well as two novels, five verse novels and several other works. Among his awards is the ACU Poetry Prize for 2017. His latest books include *The Best Australian Poems 2014* and *2015* (as editor), *Plevna: A Verse Biography of Sir Charles Ryan* (UWAP, 2016) and *Hard Horizons* (Pitt Street Poetry, 2017).

Claire Potter is author of the poetry books *Swallow* (Five Islands Press), *In Front of a Comma* (Poets Union) and *N'ombre* (Vagabond Press). She is from Western Australia.

Ron Pretty's most recent book of poetry, *The Left Hand Mirror*, was published in 2017. A revised edition of *Creating Poetry* was published by Pitt Street Poetry in 2015.

Brendan Ryan is the author of five collections of poetry. *Travelling Through the Family* (Hunter Publishers) was published in 2012 and was shortlisted for the 2014 Victorian Premier's Awards. His most recent collection is *Small Town Soundtrack* (Hunter Publishers, 2015).

Gig Ryan's *New and Selected Poems* came out in 2011 (Giramondo; Bloodaxe U.K.). She has also written songs with Disband – *Six Goodbyes* (1988), *Driving Past, Real Estate* (1999) and *Travel* (2006). She was poetry editor of the *Age* from 1998–2016, and is a freelance reviewer.

Tracy Ryan is a Western Australian writer who has also lived overseas in England, the USA & Ireland. Her ninth collection of poetry, *The Water Bearer*, is due out in 2018 (Fremantle Press), as is her fifth novel, *We Are Not Most People* (Transit Lounge).

Philip Salom lives in North Melbourne and has published fourteen books of poetry and three novels. *Waiting*, his recent novel, was shortlisted for the 2017 Miles Franklin Award and the Victorian Premier's Prize. His most recent poetry collection is the trilogy *Alterworld*.

Jaya Savige was born in Sydney, grew up on Bribie Island, Queensland, and lives in London. He is the author of *Latecomers* (UQP, 2005), which won the NSW Premier's Prize for Poetry, and *Surface to Air* (UQP, 2011), which was shortlisted for the *Age* Poetry Book of the Year and the WA Premier's Prize for Poetry. He is poetry editor for the *Australian*.

Michael Sharkey lives in Central Victoria. The author of nearly twenty collections of poetry, he earned a BA from the University of Sydney and a PhD from the University of Auckland. His poetry collections include *Alive in Difficult Times* (1991) and *Another Fine Morning in Paradise* (2012), and the collection of essays *The Poetic Eye, Occassional Writings 1982–2012* (2016).

Melinda Smith has published five books of poetry, most recently *Goodbye, Cruel* (Pitt Street Poetry, 2017). Her last book, *Drag down to unlock or place an emergency call*, won the Prime Minister's Literary Award. She is based in the ACT and is a former poetry editor of the *Canberra Times*.

Vivian Smith was born in Hobart but has lived in Sydney for many years. He has published nine collections of poetry.

Maria Takolander's most recent poetry book is *The End of the World* (Giramondo, 2014). Her poems have been widely translated and anthologised. Maria is also a prize-winning fiction writer and the author of *The Double (and Other Stories)* (Text, 2013). She is an associate professor at Deakin University in Geelong.

Andrew Taylor has published eighteen books of poems plus several other books. His poetry has been published extensively in Australia and overseas, and he currently divides his time between Sydney in Wiesbaden in Germany.

Heather Taylor Johnson is an American Australian writer living in Adelaide. Her second novel is *Jean Harley was Here* (UQP, 2017) and her fourth book of poetry is *Meanwhile, the Oak* (Five Islands Press, 2016). She is the editor of the anthology *Shaping the Fractured Self: Poetry of Chronic Illness and Pain* (UWAP, 2017).

Tim Thorne won the William Baylebridge Award in 2007, the Christopher Brennan Award in 2012 and the Gwen Harwood Prize in 2014. The latest of his fifteen collections of poetry is *Running Out of Entropy* (Walleah Press, 2017). He inaugurated and for seventeen years directed the Tasmanian Poetry Festival.

Mark Tredinnick, poet and essayist, is the winner of the Montreal Poetry Prize, the Cardiff Poetry Prize, and many other awards. His books of poetry include *Fire Diary*, *Bluewren Cantos* and *Almost Everything I Know*. Two new collections of his poetry will appear in 2018.

Todd Turner's first collection of poetry *Woodsmoke* was published by Black Pepper Publishing in 2014. The book was shortlisted for the Dame Mary Gilmore Award and the Anne Elder Award. Turner's poems have been widely published in literary journals and newspapers such as *Meanjin*, *Southerly*, *Overland* and the *Australian*.

John Upton was a professional dramatist for 27 years. He had written for more than twenty Australian television series, including *Neighbours*, and *Raffey's Rules*. His political comedy *Machiavelli, Machiavelli* won the 1985 Australian Writers Guild's award for Stage – Original Work. He had five stage plays produced over his career as a professional writer.

Chris Wallace-Crabbe is the author of two-dozen books of poetry, here and overseas. Son of a journalist, he was raised to 'be interested in everything'. His latest books are *My Feet Are Hungry* (Pitt Street Poets) and *Afternoon in the Central Nervous System* (George Braziller). Fanatically outdoorish, he has been characterised as 'a smuggler of surprises'.

John Watson has lived in the Blue Mountains for the past forty years. He has had published forty books, all of which he recommends without reservation. Many are small enough to be carried in the hand with a mobile device, enabling them to be read in periods of inactivity during recharging. Poetry must adapt.

Alan Wearne retired from the University of Wollongong at the end of 2016 and now lives in Melbourne. His Grand Parade Poets has published *With The Youngsters*, a collection of Group Sestinas and Group Villanelles his classes composed for over eighteen years.

Petra White's most recent collection is *Reading for a Quiet Morning* (Gloria SMH, 2017).

Jessica L. Wilkinson is the author of *Marionette: A Biography of Miss Marion Davies* (2012) and *Suite for Percy Grainger* (2014), both with Vagabond Press. She teaches creative writing at RMIT University.

Chloe Wilson is the author of two poetry collections, *The Mermaid Problem* and *Not Fox Nor Axe*, which was shortlisted for the Kenneth Slessor Prize and the Judith Wright Calanthe Award. She received equal first prize in the 2016 Josephine Ulrick Poetry Prize, and was shortlisted for the 2017 Commonwealth Short Story Prize.

Fiona Wright's latest collection of poetry is *Domestic Interior* (2017). Her first collection, *Knuckled*, won the 2012 Dame Mary Gilmore Award; and her book of essays *Small Acts of Disappearance* won the 2016 Kibble Award and the Queensland Literary Award for non-fiction, and was shortlisted for the Stella Prize.

'**Rae Desmond Jones** (1941–2017) made a big contribution to Australian poetry. Wherever necessary his lean, no nonsense verse courted the unacceptable, wore its heart on its sleeve, whilst always enjoying the associated risks. To those underrating or ignoring Rae, the loss is yours.' —Billy Ah Lun